Women Pioneers IN Oriya Literature

Dr. SAVITRI ROUT, M.A., Ph. D.
Reader and Head of the Department of Sanskrit,
Ravenshaw College, Cuttack.

MOTILAL BANARSIDASS
DELHI :: PATNA :: VARANASI

Head Office : BUNGALOW ROAD, JAWAHARNAGAR, DELHI-7
Branches : 1. CHOWK, VARANASI (U.P.)
2. ASHOK RAJ PATH (OPP. PATNA COLLEGE), PATNA-4 (BIHAR)

First Edition 1971
Second Revised Edition 1972
Price Rs. MLBD Rs 95.00

Printed in India

BY SHANTILAL JAIN, AT SHRI JAINENDRA PRESS, BUNGALOW ROAD, JAWAHARNAGAR, DELHI-7 AND PUBLISHED BY SUNDARLAL JAIN, FOR MOTILAL BANARSIDASS, BUNGALOW ROAD, JAWAHARNAGAR, DELHI-7

PROLOGUE

I am indebted to Messrs. Cuttack Students' Store for supplying me with all the reference books from which I have collected materials for writing out this 'monograph'. My special thanks are due to Sri Anant Misra, Proprietor, Cuttack Students' Store for publishing my monograph entitled 'Oriyā Sāhityare Nārī Prativā' in Oriya which inspired me to write another one in English entitled 'Women Pioneers in Oriya Literature'; but due to unavoidable circumstances the Oriya book could not be released to the market, though it was published two years ago.

On the eve of the simultaneous release of the two books to the market, I pray for the grace of God, the blessings of my revered teachers and goodwill of both of the publishers.

AUTHOR

Ancient Prayer of the Scholar

From the cowardice that shrinks from new truth,
From the laxness that is content with half-truth,
From the arrogance that thinks it knows all truth,
Oh ! God of Truth, deliver us.

Reader's Digest
September, 1966

"Sailing After Knowledge"

"Literature is the most significant record of men's struggles which we possess."

Edmund Wilson

[*American literary critic, historian, novelist, short story writer, social reporter and chronicler.*]

x x x x

"The hand that rocks the cradle is the hand that rules the world."

W. R Wallace

[*John O' London's Treasure Trove*]

CONTENTS

LIST OF ILLUSTRATIONS

Endorsement

I had the pleasure to supervise the presentation, contents and the scheme of the *monograph* 'Women Pioneers in Oriya Literature' by Dr. Savitri Rout during the tenure of her Post-Doctorate fellowship under the auspices of the University Grants' Commission.

Vani Vihar
10-6-70

Sd./- P. Pradhan
Professor of Sanskrit
Utkal University, Vani Vihar

AUTHOR'S NOTE

The main feature of this monograph is an elaborate essay on poetesses and women writers of Orissa, ancient and modern, who have won recognition in their respective fields. I do not know if I am competent enough to write anything on the poetry composed by the women of Orissa in the Oriya language, since I cannot claim myself to be a recognised poetess in the true sense of the term. When something most inspiring happens, one's emotions may for a time be roused to the level of feeling as that of a poet's, but such feelings will not enthuse one to write poetry, unless one is 'poetically gifted. These poetical gifts are inborn in a man or woman, they cannot be cultivated by practice. One needs the gift to write poetry combining it with one's own depth of feelings and a sense of elaborate imagination. I cannot venture to brag about myself to be in possession of such a creative touchstone which shapes the total personality of a 'poetess'. Hence the present work is rather a compilation of the views and reviews of my predecessors, who have worked in this specialised field, supplemented by an anthology of quotations from the poems or other compositions of such authors.

In spite of my limitations, the primary idea of compiling such a piece was in my mind, on being requested a decade ago by the authorities of the Utkal University. An occasion for writing such a monograph arose, when an 'Introduction' for my main work, the edition of the Sanskrit drama 'Puruṣottama Deva' by Mādhavi Dāsī, was needed. Mādhavī Dāsī, a Vaiṣṇavī poetess of the Middle Era of Oriya literature, seems to be the first and foremost woman-writer of Orissa. Her works are preserved in the different Museums of India. To judge the talents of Mādhavī Dāsī properly, she has been put in the background of both the ancient and modern periods for comparison and contrast. Her importance counts all the more, since she seems, uptil now, to be the only Oriya woman dramatist of a Sanskrit play—'Puruṣottama Deva'. There might have been other Sanskrit dramas composed by women in Orissa, but unfortunately such works have not been discovered till the present day.

In a comprehensive work of criticism, the acts of commissions and omissions are apt to occur. Hence I expect, in the words of Joseph Wood Krutch—"No one, I hope, will accuse me of being biased or unfair. Or rather I hope that no one will fail to understand that in order to make a point which I believe to be worth making, I have permitted myself to be both biased and unfair—at least in so far as my presentation of only one side of a case is inevitably unfair." At the same time, I have allowed my morals to be weighed in equal balance with my analytical acumen. If my comments directly or indirectly injure anybody's sentiments, I beg to be excused, for it is not my intention to hurt anybody. To be more precise, I aim at constructive criticism, rather than a destructive one. To me all poets and writers, living or non-living, acquainted or unacquainted are but one pouring out their hearts to me, in which I find an identification of their feelings with those of mine :

Although I never heard your name
And hardly saw your face
You poured out all your heart to me.
As we kept pace.

Wilfred Gibson

For the commissions, I have already explained my stand; as to the omissions, which are yet to be pointed out, I beg an advance apology and when such omissions will be communicated to me, I will be very glad to accommodate them in the subsequent editions of my book.

The quotations from the Oriya books have been translated into English by me. Being a Sanskritist, I claim no authority in the English language ; hence I beg to be excused by their authors if there is any flaw in such translations to convey the meanings in their proper perspective or context.

The unpublished writings of some poetesses preserved in the Orissa State Museum, though not less important, have not been taken into account here. Also some artistically flowery compositions which have withered away without the sustenance of their identified writers have not filled the basket of my collections. I express my sincere regret for not being able to bring forth such worthy writers into lime-light.

Finally, I take this opportunity to thank the following authorities, authors, scholars and the publishers for lending me a helping hand in bringing out a successful presentation. They are—

(i) Sm. U. Lakshmikanthamma, member, Andhra Sahitya Akademy and Kendriya Sahitya Akademy for inspiring me to write out this monograph not only by sending a printed 'Manifesto' to me, but also writing to me a note of appreciation, after the publication of the first edition of this monograph.

(ii) Sri R. N. Das, The Station Director, All India Radio, Cuttack, for permitting me to utilise in the body of my work, a series of talks broadcast by me from the A.I.R., Cuttack, under the caption, 'Oriyā Sāhityare Nārī' in the year 1958.

(iii) Prof. M. D. Paradkar, M.A., Ph.D., who has been kind enough to send me a reprint of his paper read at the Oriental Conference, 1965, from which I have quoted extracts.

(iv) Dr. Debaprasad Patnaik, M.A., Ph.D, (Louisville), my brother-in-law and Reader in English, Ravenshaw College, Cuttack, for the necessary suggestions as regards the English language.

(v) Dr. Gour Kishore Das, M.A., Ph.D. (Cantab.), Reader in English, Delhi University, for introducing me to Messrs Motilal Banarsidass, the publishers, who took up the publication of my monograph very promptly in spite of their heavy engagements.

"*Let noble thoughts come to us from every side*"
Rigveda 1-8-91

Ravenshaw College,
Cuttack.
10. 6. 1971

[illegible] Maulvi [illegible] for the [illegible] of [illegible]

[illegible]

(8) Prof. [illegible] Sanskrit [illegible] College [illegible]

[illegible]

I

EVOLUTION OF THE STATUS OF WOMEN IN SOCIETY

People, in general, have a wrong impression in their minds as to the real position of women in Ancient India. It is perhaps due to their ignorance of the original Sanskrit texts of the *Śrutis* and *Smṛtis*, which throw a great deal of light as regards the high status of women in the then society.

To quote some authorities—

"Women in ancient India occupied a dignified place. They participated in the outdoor life as circumstances and situation demanded and there were hardly any prescribed positions exclusively earmarked for men."[1] "All the high avenues of learning were open to women. During this period we come across a reference to some women who excelled in learning and their hymns are included in the highly prized *Vedas*. The women who could continue these studies throughout their life are known as *Bramhavādinīs*. Some of the outstanding women of that age were *Lopāmudrā*, *Apālā*, *Kadru*, *Ghoṣā*, *Paulomī* and others. The notable philosopher of the time was Gārgī."[2]

"The Buddhists maintained the tradition of Brahmanical religion and gave an honoured place to women in the social life of the country. Women were admitted into the order of

1. (i) History of Dharma Śāstra, Ancient and Mediaeval Religions and Civil Law (Poona), Vol. II, Part I : by Dr. P. V. Kane, p. 556.
   (ii) Hindu Civilisation by Radha Kumud Mukherjee, 1936, p. 73.
   (iii) Role of Women in the Freedom Movement, 1857-1947, by Manmohan Kaur—Preface.
2. (i) The Position of Women in Hindu Civilisation from Pre-historic time to the Present day : by A. S. Altekar, p. 13.
   (ii) Role of Women in Freedom Movement, 1857-1947 by Manmohan Kaur—Preface.

Nuns by virtue of which they gained opportunities to learn and to serve. They participated in the public life and won distinctions. Many a woman left lives of wealth and ease and took up missionary work. Prominent among them were *Dharmapālā*, *Annapūrṇā*, *Queen Kherā*, *Champā* and others"[1]

Women continued enjoying the same status in Indian society until the Muslim invasions. The political instability and terrors following such attacks forced women to use '*Purdah*', which retarded their intellectual progress. After the British occupation and settlement, the status of women in society improved, though they still remained a prominent theme for satirical criticism.

Evolution of Literature :

In the greater part of India today "languages are spoken which are derived from a single form of speech which was introduced into India by invaders from the North-West more than three thousand years ago. The invading peoples were known in their own language as *Ārya*, a word which is also commonly used as an adjective meaning 'noble, honourable'. Behind them, in Central Asia remained kindred peoples who eventually occupied the plateau of Iran, as well as large tracts of Central Asia. These peoples used the same name of themselves, in *Avestan*—airya, and from the genetive plural of this word the modern name *Irān* is ultimately derived. In conformity with this usage, the *Āryan* is now used as the common name of these peoples and their languages; alternatively the term Indo-Irānian is commonly used. To distinguish the Indian branch from the *Irānian*, the term *Indo-Āryan* has been coined, and as applied to language, it covers the totality of languages and dialects derived from this source from the earliest times to the present day. It is practical to distinguish three periods, Old, Middle and Modern *Indo-Āryan*. For the classical form of the old language the native grammarians used the name '*Saṁskṛita*' meaning polished, cultivated, correct (according to the rules of grammar), in contra-distinction

1. Role of Women in the Freedom Movement, 1857-1947 by Manmohan Kaur—Preface.

to *Prākṛita*, the speech of the uneducated masses, which was the same *Indo-Āryan* in origin, but was subject to a process of steady change and evolution. As a term to distinguish Indo-Āryan from the non-Āryan languages, the adjective *Ārya* was used in opposition to "*mlechha*"—"*barbarian*".[1]

The language of the '*Aryan*' was such '*Saṁskrita*' in which were composed the *Vedas*—the earliest document of Indian civilisation and culture. But this '*Saṁskṛita*' differs in its grammatical form and composition from the later '*Saṁskṛita*' which is called classical '*Saṁskṛita*'. "From the early days when hymns were chanted by the Vedic seers to the rising sun in the east, to the shining fire on the altar, to the thundering clouds above, we find in literary compositions contemporary life and thoughts. The Vedic hymns are the earliest known Sanskrit literature. Therein do observation, sympathy and surprise play the most important part. It would be a responsible supposition that after a time surprise gave place to speculation, and sympathy to study, while observation grew keener and closer."[2]

This observation is 'Literature'. 'Literature means two things—(i) Literature is life—Life understood as a vital force always working through and in relation to its surroundings. In this sense literature is wider in its scope as well as in its form. In trees and flowers budding in spring or fading in autumn, in rivers flowing and in seas surging, in the rustling of wind and in the singing of birds, equally as in the behaviour of man is embedded Life's literature. Life expressed, Life interpreted, Life asserted and Life made living—all this is Literature. To a man of routine life, however, such a literature is derived in its freshness. (ii) Thus arises the second meaning of Literature, i.e., the work of poets. A poet is one who has seen life as expression, accommodation and assimilation and who holds out for others, like a mirror, this vision of his. It is this mirror held, this attempt to convey one's vision to others, that constitutes literature".[3]

1. **The Sanskrit Language : by T. Burrow, p. 1.**
2. **Drama in Sanskrit Literature : by R. V. Jagirdar, p. 3.**
3. **Ibid. p. 3.**

Substitution of the word "Sāhitya" for the word "Kāvya"

Even if there is no direct evidence, it would not be entirely unjustifiable to assume that the Sanskrit Kāvya literature, highly stylised though it is, had its origin in the two great Epics of India[1]—the *Rāmāyaṇa* and the *Mahābhārata*. Thus in Sanskrit literature all the poetical compositions except the Vedas and the Epics come under the jurisdiction of the Sanskrit word 'Kāvya'. But in the *Kāvya-mīmāṁsā*' of *Rāja-śekhara* (C 9th A.D.) we find for the first time the word '*Sāhitya*' used for the word '*Kāvya*' as a synonym. Hence it seems that down from the time of the Epics the word '*Kāvya*' is being evolved to get its final shape to have its connotation in the word '*Sāhitya*'. This evolution covers a period of about one thousand years, which has been delineated by Pandit Baldev Upadhyaya in the following manner :

Bhāmaha (C 6th A. D.), the earliest of the writers in Poetics narrates the characteristics of Kāvya as follows :

Śabdārthau sahitau kāvyam
[*Kāvyālaṅkāra*]

Kāvya-śabdoyaṃ guṇālaṅkāra-
Saṃskṛitayoḥ śabdārthayor
Bhaktyā tu śabdārthamātravacanotra gṛhyate
[*Kāvyālaṅkārasūtravṛtti, I, I, I*]

Kāvya is developed out of the communion of the word (Śabda) and its meaning (Artha). Though the word '*Sāhitya*' has not been used here, still the implication of the communion of Śabda and Artha leads to the assumption—'Sahitayoḥ bhāvaḥ Sāhityam.'

Rājaśekhara (C 9th A. D.) for the first time in his '*Kāvyamīmāṁsā*'—used the word '*Sāhitya*' in the sense of Kāvya. In this connection he narrates a beautiful story in his book on Poetics. It runs thus—The marriage of *Sarasvatī's* son named '*Kāvya Puruṣa*' took place with *Sāhitya-Vidyā-Vadhū*. To quote Rājaśekhara :

1. History of Sanskrit Literature: by S.K. De. p. 1.

Pañcamī sāhityavidyā
Sā hi catasṛṇāmapi vidyānāṃ niṣyandah.
[*Kāvyamīmāṃsā*, *P*. 4]

There are four kinds of *Vidyā—Ānvīkṣikī*, *Trayī*, *Vārtā* and *Daṇḍanīti*. The fifth *Vidyā* is *Sāhitya*.

Bhojarāja (C 11th A. D.) in his *Sṛṅgāraprakāśa* states—'*Śabdārthau sahitau kāvyam*'. Then he goes on to explain it: '*Kiṃ Sāhityam*' ? '*Yaḥ śabdārthayoḥ sambandhaḥ*'. Hence, according to Bhoja the communion of *Śabda* and *Artha* is *Sāhitya*.

Kuntaka (C 10th A.D.), the pioneer of *Vakrokti* school of Poetics, defines *Sāhitya* as it stands in its modern and present connotation as :

Sāhityamanayoḥ śobhāśālitāṃ prati kāpyasau
anyūnānatiriktatva-manohāriṇyavasthitiḥ.
[*Vakroktijīvitam*—1, 17]

The presentation of the *Śabda* and *Artha* in a fascinating way devoid of 'Nyūnatā' and 'Atiriktatā' is termed as *Sāhitya*. Again he confirms it with another Śloka—

Śabdārthau sahitau vakrakavivyāpāraśālini
Bandhe vyavasthitau kāvyaṃ tadvidāhlādakāriṇi.[1]

Evolution of Oriya Language :

As regards the evolution of the Oriya language, Dr. Suniti Kumar Chatterjee, National Professor, puts forward his view :

"The oldest contemporary documents of the fully formed Oriya language go back to the second half of the 13th century in Lakhsmi Narasimha temple at Simachalam, but the language there is halting and not yet fully developed".[2] In continuation

1. "Bharatiya Sahitya Sastra; by Pandit Baldev Upadhyaya, Part—I, P. 569-70.
2. Artavallabha Mohanti Memorial Lectures, 1st series, 1964, by Dr. Suniti Kumar Chatteriee, P. 31.

he writes again—"The language has remained almost unchanged through these centuries—right down to the 20th. This is a very remarkable thing about Oriya among all the New Indo-Aryan languages, except perhaps, to some extent, in the case of Sindhi. Similarly, amongst the Romanic languages of Europe derived from Latin (paralleling the development of the New Indo-Aryan speeches from old Indo-Aryan or Sanskrit), Italian alone is most conservative, compared with its sister-speeches French, Provencal and Catalonian, Spanish, Portuguese and Rumanian, and presents almost the same speech as in the 13th century. The sound-system of Oriya does not seem to have undergone any great modification from the 12th century or earlier. Even in the matter of the final vowels, Oriya has retained them right down to the present day. Already from about 1400 A. D. Bengali, and possibly also Assamese, lost its final vowels. Some of the dialects of Hindi, for example Braj-Bhāshā, seemed to have kept up the final vowels upto the 17th century. But in the present day North Indian Aryan languages, except for Sindhi and Oriya, these final vowels inherited from Prakrit have almost all disappeared in pronunciation. The complicated vowel changes in Bengali and in other languages which are sisters of Oriya have never infected Oriy—excepting perhaps the epenthesis of *y*, as for example *Rājia* for Rājya. There have been comparatively fewer innovations in grammar—i. e. in morphology. So that it would be quite proper to say : if one would like to find out what Old Assamese and Old Bengali were like, one could easily get the answer from Oriya ; just as among the Germanic languages, German (or High German) has preserved much more of Primitive Germanic (except in the case of certain sounds) than English, Dutch or Scandinavian. The retention of the final vowels, particularly the medial and final *a*, has given to Oriya a certain archaic character. The elaborate system of vowel change in Bengali, the ramifications of the declensional systems in Bengali, as well as the elaborate series of personal terminations for the inflected forms of the verb, as in Bengali and in the Bihar speeches, are conspicuous by their absence in Oriya. Oriya is thus a full language based on Māgadhī, Apabhraṃśa, which was its immediate source—full in the sense that it preserved more or less intact the inflections which it inherited from Māgadhī Apabhraṃśa".[1]

"The presence of the vowels in the middle and end of words (which are generally dropped by Bengali and the rest) gives to Oriya a musical quality or character, which is no doubt archaic, but it is quite characteristic of the speech. The extraordinary development of Sabdālaṅkāra or rhetorical flourishes and figures of speech based on sound, e.g. on assonance and jingle, which characterised Oriya poetry from the 17th century onwards, became very easy for Oriya because of the language having retained a good deal of the phonetic atmosphere of Sanskrit and Prakrit, and because of the habit it developed (like Malayalam and Telugu) of borrowing Sanskrit words to saturation".[2]

Whatever may be the medium of expression, i.e. the language in which the ideas are expressed, the contribution of women to literature starts right from the Vedic period.

Contributions of Women to Ancient and Mediaeval Sanskrit Literature:

"It is interesting to note that women have been contributing to Sanskrit literature from the days of the Ṛigveda. According to tradition, 26 hymns of the Ṛigveda have been attributed to women among whom figure the names of *Romaśā* (Brahmavādinī), *Ghoṣāsūryā*, *Visvāvārā Ātreyī*, *Lopāmudrā*, *Vasukrapatnī*, *Indrāṇī*, *Apālā* (*Kanyā*), *Śraddhā* (*Kāmāyanī*), *Vaivasvatī Yamī and Vāc*. Some of these such as *Romaśā*, *Lopāmudrā* etc. are seen participating in dialogues and hence may not be given exclusive importance. The hymn attributed to *Indrāṇī* (X. 145) is of the nature of a spell against the influence of a co-wife. Here *Indrāṇī* speaks of digging out a herb which will be effective in harming the co-wife and getting the undivided attention of the husband. Although the hymn emphasises '*sapatnīṃ me parā dhama*' and '*patiṃ me kevalaṃ kuru*,'

1. Artavallabha Mohanti Memorial Lectures, 1st Series, 1964. by Dr. Suniti Kumar Chatterji, pp. 43-44.
2. Ibid p. 45.

its poetic quality need not be lost sight of as it is rounded off with telling illustrations contained in :

"*Māmanu pra te mano vatsam gauriva dhāvatu pathā vārīva dhāvatu.*"

"The well known *Apālā-Sūkta* (wherein *Apālā* is referred to as *Kanyā*) speaks of a girl suffering from skin-disease, who, coupled with devotion, successfully invokes to her favour God Indra who surmounts all difficulties in her way."

In continuation the author states—

"Stray verses from different anthologies throw light on the fact that 33 poetesses have written good poems. Rājaśekhara himself informs us about *Prabhudevī Lāṭī* who was,—

Sūktīnāṃ smarakelīnaṃ kalānām cha vilāsabhūḥ

as well as one *Vijayāṅkā* who was taken to be the abode of *Vaidarbhī* Rīti after Kālidāsa."[1]

The literary composition of Oriya poetesses of the later decadent period of Sanskrit, when Oriya was accepted both as spoken and written language, formed independently a small and unpretentious branch, as distinguished from the literary compositions of their meritorious male contemporaries such as *Sāralā Dās*, *Upendra Bhañja*, *Fakirmohan*, *Rādhānāth* or *Madhusūdan*. Such a branch was composed in verses which were easier to memorise and could be utilised for condensed and effective expression, when reproduced. These writings were exclusive monopolies of women in the feminine world, which roughly fell into three periods, corresponding to the compositions of their male counterparts :

(1) The Ancient age (Folk literature or Sāralā literature)

(2) The Middle age (Vaiṣṇava and Rīti or Alaṅkāra literature.)

1. Reproduced from the Paper read at the All-India Oriental Conference, 22nd Session at Gauhati, Assam, 1965, by Prof. M. D. Paradkar.

(3) The Modern age (Modern literature and ultra-modern literature.)

According to the observation of Sri S. N. Dash, (a scholar in Oriya Literature) the dates of this age-division can be approximately fixed as follows :

The Ancient age—C 11th to C 16th A. D.
The Middle age—C 16th to C 19th A. D.
The Modern age—C 19th—Continuing.

II

THE ANCIENT AGE

In matters of expression the ancient Oriya mind has always preferred poetry to prose. The folk songs of this period command attention, not only by their interesting narrative content, but also the works show a sense of value of the simple and direct style, which we rarely find in the heavily constructed and dexterously stylistic Kāvyas of the later period.

"Folk-songs constitute the essential part of oral literature of a society. They are the songs which a layman can easily understand and appreciate. They contain simple language and convey age-old ideas. Those songs are not the exclusive property of any individual but they are considered as national heritage for which anybody of the society can feel proud of. Their authorship cannot be traced to any particular individual."[1]

The first authentic attempt at collecting the Oriya folk-songs was done by Prof. Dr. Kunjabehari Dash and Sri Chakradhar Mohapatra. Commenting on such collections Pandit Suryanarayan Dash writes—"Some of them might have sprung up at the early stage of development of Oriya language. Till the period of rule of the Gaṅga dynasty (1042 A. D. to 1435 A. D.) many of them were perhaps in vogue."[2]

About the importance of folk-songs, Dr. Kunjabehari Dash says "Folk songs are more ancient than even the Vedic hymns. In fact, they have originated from the very beginning of language. From that time onwards people are singing the folk-songs. In the Vedic age folk-songs were sung at the time of child-birth, initiation ceremony, marriage etc. We get proofs of this from the Vedas themselves. In course of time intellectual literature and folk literature began to run in parallel. Each one was influenced by the other. Sometimes

1. Marriage and Kinship as depicted in Andhra Pradesh by N. V. Kameswara Rao—Folklore, November, 1970.
2. Oriya Sahityara Itihāsa, Part I by Pandit Suryanarayan Dash, p. 40. (Trans. by me)

intellectual literature came down to the level of folk-literature and sometimes folk-literature climbed up to the status of intellectual compositions. The first and foremost poet of Oriya literature is not a learned scholar—he is a ploughman. He is the first one to attempt to compose Oriya literature in the frame-work of folk-songs."[1]

The importance of folk-songs in Oriya literature is also corroborated by the opinion of Pandit Nilakanth Das—"By literature one understands a collection of writings. But in the development of Oriya literature, these writings are not all in all. We have to search for the personality and life of the Oriyas through the medium of these writings. Hence in the process of gradual evolution of civilisation we have to spot out the essential characteristics of Oriya literature from amongst aforesaid literature and folk-tales."

To define folk-lore—

"Folk-lore comprises of tales, lullabies, proverbs, songs, rhymes, customs, superstitions, rituals, festivals etc. The totality of folk-lore contributes enormously towards the reconstruction of the cultural history of a nation. The dynastic historians attempt to draw a chronological picture—who naturally present a picture of the upper stratum. Cultural historians only penetrate into the bottom of society to collect relevant materials for peoples' history."[2]

The women-folk of Orissa composed such songs which have been preserved by oral transmission from generations to generations and thus they subscribe to a rich heritage of the cultural history of the Oriya people. It is not possible to deal with all such songs, hence a selected few will be discussed with quotations.

Lullabies and Nursery rhymes

For the greater part of the day a child jumps about and plays around. In the evening, tired and exhausted, it returns

1. Oriya Lokageeta O Kahani by Dr. K. B. Dash, p. 16-17. (Trans. by me).
2. Historical Approach to Folklore Study by Dulal Chowdhury—Folklore, Sept. 1970.

to the lap of its mother. The mother washes and feeds the child, and puts it to sleep in the bed. To induce sleep quickly she takes recourse to the singing of ballads. Perhaps the earliest inspiration in women to compose poetry originated from their desire to put the children to sleep in comfort. In such a case, the woman composes rhymes after her own sweet will, without caring for any rules or regulations of prosody. In the words of Dr. K. B. Dash—"These compositions, whatever they may be, are eternally new or old Vedic hymns as it were."

The mother bestows on her child the sweetest of her heart's blessings, for the child is the fulfilment of her youth's penance performed at the altar of her husband's love. Hence the lullabies are the expression of such affection. The natural poet and musician dwelling in the innermost heart of the child realises the value of this primeval literature so to say. Through the medium of these songs, the natural tie of affection between the mother and the child is tightened."[1]

Those songs are:

'Dhore bāiā dho
Jeu kiarīre gahala māṇḍiā
Sehi kiarīre śoa'.

Get away, you wandering creature,
Go and sleep in the field where the
Crops of Māṇḍiā have grown profusely.

Through the melody of this song the child is put at ease by the mother after turning away the man wandering at will who can carry away the naughty child from its mother if he so desires. Fantasies such as those imaginative poems are the normal aspects of a child's thinking. Some are of the opinion that fantasies are something of fear-complex in the child. But according to psychologists, fantasies must be kept alive, until the child's intellectual development is such that it can be engaged in sound creative thinking.

1. Oriya Lokageeta O Kahani by Dr. K. B. Dash, p. 210 (Trans. by me).

Such songs are poured out from a mother's heart in spontaneous response to the surging emotions and feelings, owing to her overwhelming affection towards the child. Not only the mothers of Orissa, but all mothers of all parts of the world, cannot resist this overwhelming flow of affection expressed in lullabies and nursery rhymes.

The English mother sings—

Sleep, sleep
Sleep lightly, though—
For birds do so,
Rocked by great boughs to and fro;
With wind in their feathers,
their dreams have wings,
And they visit the gardens of fabulous kings.

T. Sturge Moore.

In these lullabies one witnesses the fairies from folklore and deities from ancient mythology; philosophy and nonsense; naturalism and supernaturalism; and colloquial prose mixed with lyric verse. On the wing of the fairy queens the child is carried to the ever joyous and happy fairyland till its drowsy eyelids are closed in restful sleep.

The Oriya lullabies were mainly the composition of Oriya women gifted with poetic power; but on account of the non-availability of records as to the names of the earliest composers, we cannot ascertain with certainty from what period such compositions came into existence. Anyway, these women, though unidentified, seem to be the torch-bearers of the feminine literature.

Marriage Songs :

The gay and bright atmosphere of marriage festivity disappears at the time of bidding farewell to the bride. The parents, though happy for having secured a worthy husband for their daughter, feel heavy at heart at the time of parting. The mother specially is overwhelmed with grief and pours forth her grief in the form of loud lamentations. Apart from women, even self-restrained sages are not able to abstain from shedding tears at the time of parting with their daughters in marriage, e.g. the sage Kaṇva in the *Abhijñānaśākuntala*, while bidding farewell to her daughter *Śakuntalā* on her way to her husband Duṣyanta's capital, laments in the śloka—

> "*Śakuntalā goes to-day, my heart with*
> *anguish is met,*
> *Throat's choked with flow of tears, eyes by*
> *grief impotent.*
> *If such heavy grief's load bear, I, mere forester,*
> *How much more householder parted from her daughter.*"

(Reproduced from the "Dramas of Kālidāsa" by Bela Bose).

In later ages, such songs of wailings were considered as lyrics of self-expression of the women who could never give vent to their feelings otherwise. Women, in general, being oppressed by the dictates and the rules of society, have to repress their creative needs. Hence, though they become very conforming and obedient to the elders, specially to the mothers-in-law, they develop a sort of neurotic conflict within the range of their own minds. Ultimately, the shy and sensitive women may transform society's ridicule and dislike for them into rhythms of great beauty through the medium of loud lamentation. Out of this conflict between expression and repression the individual translates her own ideas into a language relevant to others nurtured out of such a hostile environment. Hence in between her sobs rhythmic poetry is poured forth with "good ideas accompanied by wild, silly and sometimes thoughtful metaphors."

The bride, owing to her fear-complex for the mother-in-law, tries her best to express herself by singing—

> "*Mīna kheluthāye jala bhitare lo bou,*
> *Muhiñ kheluthāi tora kolare lo bou,*
> *Dhībara jālare mina padai lo bou,*
> *Jala-krīḍā tāra sariṇa galā lo bou.*"

The fish was playing inside the water at its ease. I was also playing in your lap. Just as a fisherman catches hold of a fish in his net, I have been caught.

This implies that a girl who used to move about freely in her parents' house, is now restricted in her behaviour and movements.

To illustrate another one :

"*Duba badhuthilā kākoara khāi lo bou,*
Badhuthāi muhiñ to sneha pāi lo bou,
Kruṣna māyā kale Gopiṇka pāiñ lo bou,
Bāpā māyā kale mohari pāiñ lo bou."

(Oriya Sāhityara Itihāsa—Part I, By Pandit Suryanarayan Dash, P. 55.)

The Duba grass grows by the sprinkling of dew drops. The daughter grows up in the affectionate lap of her mother. Just as Śrīkṛiṣṇa, by means of deceptive trick, deceived the Gopīs, has father indulged in such a practice by sending me away ?

Gradually their songs became a convention to be sung on the occasion of the daughter's departure to the bridegroom's home. Such conventions began to be practised with great gusto and regular teachers were appointed to train up the daughters of marriageable age in the art of wailing aloud. In spite of their aesthetic attraction and spiritual values such compositions could never attain the status of intellectual literature; they gained popularity amongst the women-mass. Till the present day such practice is still to be found in the interior parts of villages, where the light of western civilisation has not dawned yet.

Proverbial couplets :

The use of proverbial couplets are quite common in the feminine world. Some of them are used to produce humour, some for quotations, and some for enjoyment of simple jokes. Sometimes when the village women have a quarrel, they use some selected proverbs as a part of their abusive language. Such couplets are specifically classed as "taunting couplets." Morals and essential truths are expressed through such proverbs in a concise form so as to appeal readily to the mass mind of illiterates.

Ati serentāre serentā jhia kaande nā
Chāula pachhake khāibā bhāta raandhe nā
Ati serentāre serentā pua kaande nā
Gāli chāripada sahibā pachhake gāī bāndhe nā

(A desire to eat the neighbour's crops raised in the cornfield)

My dear daughter, do not weep,
Do not cook, let us eat even unboiled rice
My dear son, do not weep,
Do not fetter the cow, even though we will be reproached.

Daśa doṣa jadi sahi pāribu
bohu āṇibu gharaku
Hasī kari jadī kathā kahibu
baśa karibu paraku.
(A favourite of all)

If you can tolerate ten faults then
bring a bride to your house
If you can talk laughingly
you can subdue the enemy.

Taunting proverbs :—

Kahi jāuthāu sinā
Tuhāi tuhāi puṭa deuthile
Luhā ki hoiba sunā

Even if you babble a lot, can iron be turned to gold with the application of paints ?

Akhāi karichhi oṣā
Dolika chāula olike khāichhi
Dāntā achhi daraghaṣā.

She has observed fast but has already taken a lot of rice in the previous night, though she has not washed her face (in the morning).

[Oriyā Prahelikā Saṃgraha—by Batakrishna Praharaj p. 70-93]

Songs of Festivities :

In the remote villages of Orissa, the pleasure of living, labour and enjoyment are understood. There in the open sun-bathed fields, through wild jungles, across rugged paths, up and down the silvery streams, the highways and byways, one can still hear the sweet music of rustic melodies whose appeal strikes at the very soul, specially in the silent stillness of tropical moonlit-night. For such enjoyments women observe fasts (in corresponding Oriyā language it is called Oṣā) which end with celebrations, festivities and sumptuous home-made refreshments. Though these festivals occur all throughout the year, the major ones amongst them are celebrated during the months of July to December, when the male-partners of the village women are comparatively free from their duty of cultivation. Each fast or Oṣā is performed in conformity with a symbolic story behind its observance. On auspicious occasions like this, village women get ample opportunities to compose songs and by singing them can demonstrate their inborn faculty for poetical compositions. The important ones amongst them are—

Swing-paddling songs :

These songs are sung on the occasion of the 'Rāja' festival, as it is known in the popular Oriya language. It is celebrated consecutively for three days beginning from *Māsānta* and continuing upto *Mithuna Saṅkrānti* and *Mithuna Niraṁśa Day* in the month of *Āṣāḍha.* The symbolical story behind it is that Mother-earth menstruates for three days before her tilling for the production of crops begins. This festival is specifically observed by unmarried girls and women. Mother-earth is allowed to relax during this period of her menstruation. So no soil is tilled, no vegetables are chopped in the house, no spices are grinded and practically manual labour comes to a standstill. Even women do not walk bare-foot on the floor; they use the sheaths of plantain trees as a sort of slippers on their feet. The children play various kinds of country games, specially "*Bāgudi*". Wearing of new garments is a *must* on this occasion. Various kinds of cakes are prepared on this occasion, amongst which *baked cakes* (*poḍa pītha*) are a speciality. The women-folk, specially the young unmarried girls with painted sandal paste on their fore-head, lac-dye on their feet and a lot of local cosmetics applied to their faces, with their new *sarees* on, jingle about, with their silver anklets keeping pace with the mellow movement. The colour and rhythm add to the romantic charm of the festival.

Such maidens get up on the swings hung from the huge branches of trees and begin to paddle them to the accompaniment of lilting music :

Jāre, mana doli udi jā—
Jāre, megha chhuiñ pheriā—
Basumatī mā sāradhā kathā megha deśe kahiā—

Oh ! you mental-swing, go and touch the clouds and then come away. Go and tell the clouds about our affection towards the Mother earth.

Such a panorama of settings on the back-drop of the moving swings as forest glades, vast fields, green trees, creepers and flowers sprinkled with drizzling silvery drops of rain make the young maidens' life interesting and eventful for all these three days, breathing an air of aesthetic eroticism.

Hence she sings again apprehending that she will be no more in her father's place in near future and the pleasurable thoughts of her maidenhood days, specially the spiced betel-leaf preparation (pāna in the Oriya language) will be a sweet remembrance.

Ālupatar ki sārupatara
Kebe ki hoibo-pāna?
Miliba ki āu rajaparaba
Sarile kuañri dīna?
Āsa lo āsa kuañri jhia hajijibā gītare—

Will ever potato leaves or *saru* leaves be turned to betel leaves? Shall we ever get the pleasure of these maidenhood days? Hence let us be drowned in these songs.

Khudurukuṇi Songs :

This festival is observed for propitiating goddess *Maṅgalā* or *Śakti*. Basing on the tragic story of the girl named 'Taapoi', this festival is observed. On account of its universal popularity, it is quite possible that the original story in prose has been rendered into poetry.

The story of *Taapoi* runs like this :

A rich merchant had seven sons and seven daughters-in-law. A daughter named Taapoi was born to the merchant after the sons. One day a widow, living nearby, seeing the wealth and prosperity of the merchant became envious and told the girl while at play that being the daughter of a rich merchant, she should play with a golden moon and silver basket. The child thus provoked went and asked her parents for them. But before Taapoi's coveted objects were ready for use, her parents died. The sons of the merchant in the meantime, took the responsibility of the business into their own hands and sailed out into the sea for trade. During their absence, all the six daughters-in-law except the seventh one, manipulated to drive away Taapoi to the forest. While wandering in the deep forest, Taapoi tumbled over something which afterwards she recognised to be the image of goddess *Maṅgalā*. Hence she began to worship the image with the '*Khuda*' (particles of rice) supplied to her by the youngest daughter-in-law and tied to the end of her *saree*. Fortunately the trader brothers, while returning from trade discovered Taapoi in the forest. On reaching home, they cut down the noses of all the daughters-in-law except that of the youngest as a punishment. In embarrassment these women went away to the nearby forest and were devoured by tigers. New brides were brought to the household and all of them lived happily ever after."[1]

Since the maiden Taapoi worshipped goddess *Maṅgalā* with '*Khuda*' (particles of rice) the festival is known as *Khudurukuṇi* festival. In order to get a brother's affection as Taapoi got and also for the welfare of their brothers, the unmarried sisters observe this fast.[2]

Now-a-days the images of the goddess *Maṅgalā* are being sold in the market for the purpose of worship. The worship days fall in four or five Sundays of the month of Bhādrava. Printed books are available in which verses pertaining to the tragic story of Taapoi are recorded. These verses are recited at the time of such worship:

Śuṇa sujane dei eka chitta
Ethu ante Taapoi charita

× × ×

Swāmi taparu pheribe niśchaya
Tora garbhati hoiba udaya.
Sehi garbhare hebaṭi kumārī
Tapa prabhābaru nāma tāhārī
Taapoi se nāma bolāiba
Bistāriba se tapara prabhāba

(Bṛihat *Taapoi* Oṣā By Batakṛishna Nath Sarma, P. 1-5)

Ye gentlemen, now listen to the story of Taapoi.

× × ×

After the return of your husband you will conceive. Then a daughter will be born to you. She will be called by the name of *Taapoi* and she will spread the power of meditation (Tapas).

1. Adapted from Oriya Sahityara Itihāsa : By Dr. Mayadhar Mansinha, pp. 82-83 (Trans. by me)
2. Ibid, P. 83.

Kumaraulsavba—1963

Courtesy—Smt. Yasodhara Das.

Kumāra-Pūrṇimā Songs :

This festival is observed by young unmarried girls in order to get a young husband as handsome as God *Kumāra* or '*Kārttikeya*', for there were days when the young girls were scared of the idea of getting an old widower as a husband. Hence they used to observe this fast and worship the Moon-God as a symbol of the God *Kumāra* representing youth and beauty. The auspicious day for such worship was chosen to be the full-moon day of the latter part of the month of *Āśvina*. The young maidens being kissed by the silvery moon-beams darting forth from the crystal-clear autumnal sky forget for a moment the grim realities of life. Overwhelmed by a feeling of love and romance, the whole atmosphere is charged with an *El Dorado gleam*.

The Moon God is worshipped as soon as it comes up to the evening sky. So goes the saying that if the moon gets old, i.e., if it becomes late evening for worship the worshipper gets an old husband. *Jahni* flower (a seasonal yellow flower which blossoms in the evening) and fried rice (*Khai* in the local Oriya language) and various other fruits and flowers are used for the materials of worship. But the dainty lily flower, described as the consort of the Moon God by classical Sanskrit poets forms the major ingredient of worship. A half moon is prepared out of crushed fried rice and the Pūjā floor is decorated with various works of arts (*Chitā*) sketched out by the young maidens with their own skill for the special occasion.

The maidens themselves conduct this Pūjā. For such worship no priest is called in. Just like the chanting of 'Om' in the Vedas, the 'Hulu-Huli' sound from the lips of the maidens acts as the *mantras* of the Vedas.

With such 'Hulu-Huli' sound the Moon God is propitiated by exhibiting burning earthen lamps placed in brass plates.

After this Pūjā, the maidens resort to '*Puchi Khela*.' This *Puchi Khela* is a kind of group-dance performed by the village women. The feet and hands move in the rhythm of each stepping. While playing, the flowers in the clasps of their palms become scattered.[1] This special kind of dance has also got a

1. Oriya Lokageeta O Kahani by Dr. K. B. Das, p. 200.

scientific significance behind it—

"The muscles of the thigh and the buttock are strengthened by such exercises. In future this helps in the safe delivery of the would-be mothers."[1]

The *Puchi Khela* is accompanied by such songs as—

Kuañra punei jahna go
Phuta boula venī,
Dhoba phara phara kiraṇa padichhi
Pulaki uthai mana go
Phula boula venī,
Āsa go bhauṇi māne
Ahaṅkāra śunya
Manare sebibā
Kuañara punei janha go,
Phula boulavenī,
Ethi pūji Brundābati
Phala puṣpa jāhā miliba arapi
Hoibā soubhāgyabatī go,
Phula bouḷavenī.[2]

(*Phula bouḷavenī* is an 'address' without any particular significance)

The Full-Moon of Kumāra-Pūrṇimā has come up. The white moon-light is scattered about. Oh, sisters ! come, let us worship this full-moon with a mind devoid of pride. Then we will worship 'Bṛindābatī'—We will offer the available flowers and fruits and then we will get all the blessings.

On this auspicious occasion, the maidens decorate themselves and wear bright new *sarees.* In the background of nature and natural feelings, romanticised by the presence of the snow-white lily and bright yellow *Jahni* flowers, the *Puchi-Khela* or rhythmic group dance of the young maidens sings and thrills the sentiments of the spectators– young and old alike. The particular maidens represent also all maidens and inspire the

1. Oriya Lokageeta O Kahani by Dr. K. B. Das, p. 200.
2. Sunābhāuja—Sri Hrishikesh Mohanti, p. 25.

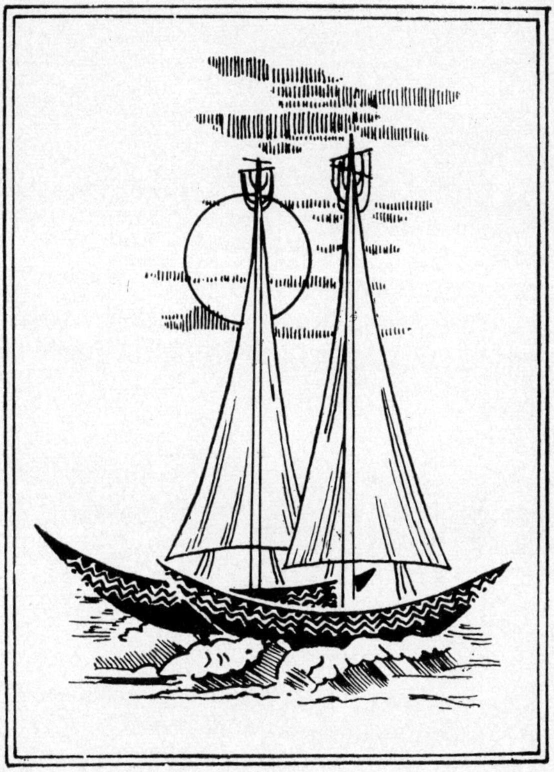

Kalinga traders (Sādhavas) setting sail on ships (Boitas)

emotional earnestness and vivid picture of the Prince-Charming of their day-dreams who is yet to come riding on a *Pakṣirāja* horse.

A modern tendency among the present day educated section of the population is an attempt to popularise the fading treasures of the 'Kumāra Pūrṇimā songs' through broad-casts in All India Radio programmes or by public stage-performances. But the attempt is sure to fall short of the expectations, since it is impossible to recapture the balance, rhythm or romantic fervour of the actual 'Pūjā floor' where such festivities take place.

Ship felicitation songs:

In ancient days the kingdom of Kalinga (the present Orissa) was famous for its maritime trade. The merchants used to go to distant islands of Sumātrā, Jāvā, Bāli etc. by ships. The traditional story identifies the present field of '*Bāli yātra*' in the city of Cuttack as the place from where the ancient traders used to set sail for the island of '*Bāli*' for trade purposes. In commemoration of this journey, every year on the *Kārttikapūrṇimā* day (the day in which the traders usually set sail for foreign islands) a fair is held over here. Goddess '*Maṅgalā*' was the presiding deity of the traders (in local Oriya language, they are called Sādhaba). Hence women worship this Goddess at the time of bidding farewell to their husbands while setting sail to the foreign islands.

But ever since the fall of Kalinga, no Oriya trader has set sail like his fore-bearers. The custom of bidding farewell to traders has also lost its original historical significance and has been converted into a custom with an interpolated religious significance added to it. Hence in the full-moon day of every *Kārttika* month, Oriya women (belonging to every caste and creed) take their purifying dip in rivers or tanks before sunrise and improvised well-decorated and well-lighted (either by candle or earthen lamps) paper-boats or, boats made out of the sheaths of plantain trees are made to float in the water by them. While pushing such boats into the water, they sing—

Ā—Kā—Mā—Bai
Pāna guā thoi
Pāna guā tora
Māsaka dharma mora.

The months ranging from *Āsāḍha* to *Kārttika* have passed out. I am offering betel and betel-nuts to you. Be you pleased with that, and in return bestow on me your meritorious virtues.

This couplet seems to be addressed to the Goddess 'Maṅgalā', who is the presiding deity in the background of such recitations.

The significance of Oriya Festivals :

As in the case of the Sinhalese, so also in ancient Orissa, popular music did not exist as rigidly separate from art. "Whatever human interest was satisfied by them, the same measure found fulfilment at every festival and ritual of an agricultural or other nature. These helped sufficiently to satisfy the emotional yearnings of men and women whose busy life afforded little leisure for the appreciation of art apart from its functional associations".[1]

All arts supplement the needs of one another, hence the simple delight derived out of Oriya folk-songs, the sublime art of sculpture at Konark, the great classical art of beauty of *Odissi* songs and dances—all these taken together, must have raised ancient Orissa to a supreme height.

Unfortunately, during the period of various invasions in Orissa, *Oḍissi* dance slipped into the precincts of houses of ill fame and degenerated steadily. The socio-cultural consciousness of the present Oriya people is providing incentive to make efforts to rejuvenate and revive the lost glory of such a magnificent dance of classical and aesthetic appeal.

A synthesis of the literature of ancient Oriya poetesses:

Once, Sri Anandashankar Ray, I.C.S., one of the famous

1. The Folk Songs of the Sinhalese by N.D.W. Jasekara, p 573.

Odissi dance by Mrs. Kum Kum Das (Mohanty) Allied Services
Courtesy—Dancer

A sculpture from Koṇārak— Accompaniment to the rhythm of music and dance.

litterateurs of both Bengal and Orissa, asked a very fundamental question to the *Nobel laureate* Poet Rabindranath Tagore, when both were out for a stroll in the morning, "Is art too good to be human nature's daily food?"[1]

To this question, we may answer that the subjective and objective compositions of women serve this purpose, for they have two distinct values in literature, one of them is the plain value of pleasure, arising out of one's own feelings and direct experience, and the other is relative value or degree to which they stimulate some new process of thinking. The writings of the former type are known as '*subjective literature*' and the latter type as '*objective literature*'. Both types are a celebration of the joys and the sorrows of life with an aesthetic value idealistically conceived. According to the Italian Philosopher Benedetto Croce, the word 'Aesthetic' is derived from the Greek word 'Aisthetikos' which means 'to perceive'. The subjective compositions of women are born out of this direct perception. Their themes are simply the disintegration and reintegration of family life revealed through their various folk-songs and also the love of the Sun, the Moon and the Earth. Such compositions are so to speak, the spontaneous outburst of a woman's aching heart, devoid of intellectual logic, which according to philosopher G. B. Vico (C. 18th A.D.) 'is not necessary in the realm of poetry'—'Poetic logic is distinguished from intellectual logic'. Poetry is a mode of consciousness or a theoretic form which precedes the philosophical or reasoning form'.[2]

Aristotle also defines this aesthetic attitude as—"The poet who feels the emotions to be described will be most convincing".[3]

Hence Croce summarises—"All the books dealing with classification and systems of art could be burnt without any loss whatever."[4]

Though there have been specimens of philosophical,

1. Rabindranath by Sri Anandashankar Ray, p. 70.
2. Scienza Nuova by G. B. Vico.
3. Aristotle's Poetry by Humphry House, p. 62.
4. Croce by Cecil Sprigge, p. 28.

intellectual and literary writings of women right from the time of the Vedas and the middle Sanskrit period, in the later decadence period, they are mainly confined to light erotic topics in the colourful embroidery of romantic fancy, or tender and touching notes in their wailings at times of great grief and sorrow or their sarcastic remarks through the proverbial couplets when they fall out with one another or their lullabies, lulling their babies to sleep or the songs sung on the festive occasions to propitiate the various personal Gods. These provide a glimpse into the hearts of women, their writings being truly feminine in outlook and presentation. Through such writings they have plucked out their bleeding hearts and then placed them on the public altar for the men to witness.

Aristotle agrees with Plato as to the theory that—'Poetry rouses the emotions'.[1] By the rousing of such emotions, the whole personality and the emotional behaviour in the real life of the reader is affected. The compositions of men are intellectual, where philosophy and reason are most powerful ; but the women let themselves loose to be carried away by their emotions and feelings. Men have never allowed 'reason' to relax its control even over such a relatively harmless part of human nature as—'the natural instinct for tears'. Men attempt even melodious poetry in a sharp practical way by producing bewilderised or didactic poetical texts. Hence, the emotions and melodies of men vary from those of the fair-sex in their interpretations. "The emotions of men are rational and restorative of the proper equilibrium in life, the balance, the mean of temperature. The melodies are—the melodies of character, the melodies of action and the orgiastic melodies." To quote Aristotle again—"They are brought back by sacred melodies to a normal condition as if they had been medically treated and undergone a catharsis." In continuation he says "And the soul of a man so affected is thus to be brought back to a balanced state."[2] The emotions of innocent joy, despair or fear arising out of women's writings are a sort of release for their emotions and a relaxation of tension.

During the period when such compositions came out

1. Aristotle's Poetics by Humphry House, p. 27.
2. Aristotle's Poetics by Humphry House—p. 107.

from the pens of women, the life of a woman in Orissa, beginning with the stage of a daughter and maturing into wifehood and motherhood, was one of constant heartache and torture. This was not only the condition in Orissa, but in the whole of India as well. To quote *Swami Vivekananda*—"The great difficulty in the Indian household is the daughter. The daughter and caste combined ruin the poor Hindu, because, you see, she must marry in the same caste, and even inside the caste exactly in the same order, and so the poor man sometimes has to make himself a beggar to get his daughter married. The father of the boy demands a very high price for his son, and this poor man sometimes has to sell everything just to go and get a husband for his daughter. The great difficulty of the Hindu's life is the daughter. And curiously enough, the word daughter, in Sanskrit is '***Duhitā***'. The real derivation is that, in ancient times, the daughter of the family was accustomed to milk the cows, and so the word '*duhitā*' comes from '*duh*'—to milk, and the word '***duhitā***' really means a *milk-maid*. Later on, they found a new meaning to that word, '***duhitā***' the milk-maid—*she who milks away all the milk of the family*. That is the second meaning."[1]

In the ancient days, sage Manu says—"A woman does not deserve independence." Bringing out a distorted meaning out of this maxim, the leaders of society and the social order of the day, prevented women from holding an independent status in society. The daughter was subjugated to the control of her parents, the wife to her husband and the mother to her son when her husband passed into the other world. This fettered existence of women in the three spheres of life as a daughter, wife and mother, prohibited her from having an independent personality or individuality, arising out of the consummation of her own thought, will and emotion. Thus the frustrated women, being unable to fulfil the innermost desire of their hearts '*to love and to be loved*' sought to find an emotional release of their pent up emotions through their own compositions.

Strangely enough, such ancient compositions conform

1. Complete Works of Swami Vivekananda—Vol. VIII—p. 66.

to the modern view of poetry. To quote George Dekker—"We do not value erudition or polished language for their own sakes in poetry; they are acceptable to us only when combined with the direct expression of real feeling. In the great volume of early Italian verse, there are many passages and some whole poems in which the words seem to us to well up from the poet's heart like fresh water from a spring. We put our finger on these passages and say—"Here is true poetry."[1]

1. (a) Shaw—p. 144.
(b) *Sailing After Knowledge* by George Dekker—p. 114.

III

THE MIDDLE AGE

The period witnesses a phase of literature arising out of the compositions of the new sect—the *Vaiṣṇava* poets of Orissa. This special branch of literature is known as '*Vaiṣṇava*' literature. Gradually this phase of composition passed on to another phase known as '*Rīti Sāhitya*' or ornamental writings in poetry towards the end of the middle age.

"Vaiṣṇavism is a technique of spiritual discipline that attempts at utilising the crude animal impulse that man inherits from the very planes of prior life, as found in many social and religious settings. It is often called the 'Natural way' inasmuch as it grounds itself on the impulses and desires with which man is born (*Saha-ja*)"[1]

Lord *Chaitanya*, being the founder of *Vaiṣṇavite* sect, is said to have lived in *Śrikṣetra* or Purī, and hence the sect also held its sway in Orissa with its five main followers who are locally named as 'Pañchasakhā.'

The doctrine of this cult preaches that the divine can be approached through a transformation of sex-impulses, described by a *Vaiṣṇava*, as a supernaturalisation of the 'natural.' A theory that may justify the use of sex-sentiments for spiritual purposes is suggested in the following account—"The true nature of the self and its relation to the Divine is revealed through the intimacies or love between *Rādhā and Kṛiṣṇa.* Such a love is intensified through many alliances between the pair of lovers and lady friends of *Rādhā*, the *sakhīs*. These latter alone can truly appreciate the depth of *Rādhā's* love for *Kṛiṣṇa*, the Divine. The true essence of Divine reality as a sense of overflowing love may, thus, be adequately appreciated through the *Sakhī*-attitude. The *sakhī* does not aim at enjoying *Kṛiṣṇa* directly, she enjoys the many love-relations between *Rādhā* and

1. A Study in Spiritual 'Leftism'—an aspect of 'Vāma-Mārga' or the 'Sahaja' cult by Prof. N.N. Sengupta—p 377. (All India Oriental Conference—12th session 1943-44)

Kṛiṣṇa."[1]

The advent of *Vaiṣṇavism* in Orissa is recorded by the historians as follows:—

"Śrī *Nimbārkāchārya*, the propounder of *Vaiṣṇava's Dvaitādvaita* doctrine in the C 12th A.D. during the reign of the rulers of the *Gaṅga* dynasty, admitted poet *Jayadeva* as one of his followers. Consequently, *Jayadeva* composed his famous *Kāvya Gītagovinda* and magnified the divine love of *Rādhā* and *Kṛiṣṇa*. Beginning from that period in many places of Orissa, monastries and temples have been erected to propitiate the dual image of *Rādha-Kṛiṣṇa*. Many poets and philosophers of Orissa have also depicted Lord *Jagannāth* himself as a representation of *Rādhā-Kṛiṣṇa*. For these reasons the lovers of ***Rādhā-Kṛiṣṇa*** carry high respect for the lord *Jagannāth*. Lord *Chaitanya* himself was enamoured by this doctrine and hence *Jagannāth's* place was very dear to him. Under the patronage of king *Pratāparudra Deva*, the depth of study in *Vaiṣṇavism of Rāya Rāmānanda*, made the then Orissa highly susceptible to the spread of the *Rādhā* and *Kṛiṣṇa* doctrine of *Vaiṣṇava* cult and the divine love of Lord *Chaitanya* nurtured by his friends and disciples helped in its wide circulation. The *Vaiṣṇava* literature composed in Oriya by the contemporaries of Śrī *Chaitanya* and afterwards, is the result of this current of *Rādhā-Kṛiṣṇa* cult.'[2]

Women played an important part in the composition of *Vaiṣṇava* literature. In fact, the *Vaiṣṇavī Mādhavī Dāsī* was the first lady to be appointed by emperor Pratāparudradeva as a 'writer' in his court. Before the reign of emperor *Pratāparudradeva*, 'Karaṇī script' was in vogue in Orissa. "A good deal of the old shapes of the letters as in the common Eastern script of a thousand years ago is still preserved in Oriya in the *chaṭā* or *uncial* or current hand as opposed to the writings in palm-leaf

1. (i) Chaitanya Charitāmṛita—Part II, Ch. 8.
   (ii) A Study in Spiritual "Leftism" an aspect of Vāma-mārga or the 'Sahaja' cult—by the Late Prof. N. N. Sengupta, Professor, Lucknow Univ. p. 377-84.
   (All India Oriental Conference—12th Session, 1943-44)
2. Oriya Sahityara Itihāsa, Prathama Bhāga, by Pandit Sūryanarayana Dash, p. 429. (Trans. by me)

Mss."[1] But afterwards, this script underwent an evolution, by which it became easier to write out the compositions in palm-leaf. This facilitated women to write out their compositions in palm leaf. "Owing to the peculiar way of writing with an iron stylus, with which letters used to be scratched on the surface of the palm-leaves, the style of writing in Orissa among the Oriya people took a new turn from after the C. 16th A. D."[2]

As historians narrate, after *Puruṣottamadeva*, Emperor *Pratāparudradeva* (1496—97 A. D.) ascended the throne of Utkala. Śrī *Chaitanyadeva* (1505 A. D. or 1510 A.D.) came to Orissa and lived in Purī. Though at times Śrī *Chaitanya* was going out on pilgrimage, altogether he lived at Purī for twenty-five years. At that time, *Balarām Dāsh*, *Jagannāth Dāsh*, *Yasobant Dāsh*, *Achyutānanda Das* and *Ananta Dāsh* known as '*Pañchasakhā*' (Five Friends) were influenced by Śri *Chaitanyadeva*. Under the patronage of *Pratāparudradeva*, with the communion of *Jñāna* and *Bhakti*—the paths of *Gauḍiya Vaiṣṇavism* began to spread, keeping *Śrī Jagannāth* as the mainspring.

"Although the Brahmins were in support of education at that time, they were not prepared to give up the traditional rules and regulations. As the *Saṁhitās* forbade the women and the *Śūdras* to take part in the discussions of the *Vedas* and *Vedāntas*, in the recitation of *Gāyatrī Mantras* and others the conservatives did not appreciate this. But on account of propagation of *Vaiṣṇava* religion, the women were not prevented from chantings, singings and worship. The Brahmins did not raise any voice of protest".[3]

This made the Oriya women come out of the sheaths of their 'Purdah' and take part in open discussions or present their various compositions. The spread of *Vaiṣṇavism* produced a new platform for the Oriya women to exhibit their talents in public, which were suppressed up till now.

1. Artaballabh Mohanti Memorial Lectures by Dr. Suniti Kumar Chatterjee, p. 46.
2. Ibid. p. 46.
3. Oriya Sahityāra Itihāsa by Pandit Suryanarayana Dash—Prathama Bhāga, p. 429. (Trans. by me)

Mādhavī Dāsī :

Mādhavī Dāsī was born in the village of *Bentapura*, in the area of *Brahmagiri*, in the district of Purī. Her cousin-brother *Rāya Rāmānanda* or *Rāmānanda Ray* was a Governor of the famous Rajmahendri, near the river Godāvarī, the Capital of South Orissa. Lord *Chaitanya* often coming to Orissa in 1520 A.D. came in contact with *Rāya Rāmānanda*. He listened with rapt attention to his discussions pertaining to the love-episode of *Rādhā Kriṣṇa* and the *Bhakti* cult. Lord *Chaitanya* was very much impressed and accepted *Rāya Rāmānanda* as one of his favourite disciples. Being widowed at an early age, *Mādhavī Dāsī* came down to her cousin-brother *Rāya Rāmānanda*, and along with her own brother, *Sikhi Mohanty*, was initiated into the doctrine of *Vaiṣṇavism* by *Śrī Chaitanyadeva*. Being born a woman, she could not be a direct disciple of *Chaitanyadeva*, because *Śrī Chaitanya* was a strict Sanyasī and did not even look at the face of women. Hence, *Mādhavī Dāsī* was accepted as a 'half-disciple'. *Chaitanyadeva* had four disciples--*Rāya Rāmānanda*, *Rūpa Gosvāmī*, *Sikhi Mohanty* (brother of *Mādhavī Dāsī*) and *Mādhavī Dāsi* herself. As *Mādhavī Dāsī* was a 'half-disciple' only, the number of disciples is counted as three and one-half. *Mādhavī Dāsī* speaks of this inhibition in her Vaiṣṇavite compositions and goes on to describe the birth of a woman to be a curse.

After this incident, *Mādhavī Dāsī* began to live in the house of her parents and began studying various literatures pertaining to religion, philosophy, *Purāṇa* and *Vaiṣṇava* literature under the supervision of her uncle *Bhavānanda Ray*. Afterwards she composed the '*Kīrtans*' in Vaiṣṇava literature. From these we get a glimpse of the emotional life of *Mādhavī Dāsī*, which is overwhelmed by the flow of *Bhakti* and devotion to God. All the compositions of *Mādhavī Dāsī* are written in '*Brajabolī*' or '*Braja bhāṣā*'. '*Brajabhāṣā*' is the dialect of the Vaiṣṇavas, which had its origin in *Śrī Bṛindāban*. Though the script is Bengali, *Brajabhāṣā* seems to have a good deal of resemblance to the Oriya language.

But unfortunately, "on account of the spread of *Vaiṣṇavism* in Orissa which in its later decadence period gave rise to looseness of character arising out of the wrong interpretation of *Vaiṣṇava* philosophy, undermined the backbone of an independent and strong nation of the Oriyas."[1] This sad tale has been narrated in the 'History of Orissa' written by Sri R.D. Banerjee, a famous historian of Bengal.[2]

In fact, such scandals were the cause of the downfall of *Mādhavī Dāsī.* A disciple of Śrī Chaitanya Deva, known as '*Chhoṭā Haridās*' came to Orissa along with *Chaitanyadeva. Mādhavī Dāsī* somehow got herself involved with this Haridās in some affairs. Śrī *Chaitanyadeva* on coming to know of this turned both of them out from the order of his *Vaiṣṇava* disciples. In mental agony, *Haridās* went back to Bengal, his home, and drowned himself in the Ganges.

On this occasion, most probably, *Mādhavī Dāsī* has written herself :

"*Je dekhale gorā mukha*
Sei preme bhāṣe
Mādhavī banchita haila
Nija karma doṣe."

Seeing the face of one with white-complexion everybody falls in love. It is only *Mādhavī Dāsī* who has been debarred on account of her bad luck.

Again, she writes in *Brajabolī* about the love-affairs of Śrī *Kṛiṣṇa*.

Chitraputhli jena bedhai sakhigaṇa
Nirakhai shyāmamukha chanda
Ki bhela ki bhela boli dhaola biṣkākhā ali
Saba jane lāgai dhanda
Śhyāmala-sundara badano-suḍhākara
Sumukhi nehārala sādhe
Upajala ullāsa kahai Mādhavī Dāsa
Bidagadha Mādhava Rādhe

1. Oriya Sahityara Itihāsa by Dr. Mayadhara Mansinha, p. 144. (Trans. by me)
2. History of Mediaeval Vaishnavism in Orissa, by P. Mukherjee p. 27.

> The hand-maids are looking at the moon-face of Śrī *Kṛiṣṇa* like a picture-post. *Viśākhā* came running telling 'How nice!' 'How nice!' *Sumukhī* (beautiful *Rādhā*) is looking at the moon-face and I, *Mādhavī Dāsī*, looking at *Rādhā-Mādhava*, am very much pleased.

Rīti Age:

The predominance of the Sanskrit Schools of poetics and their compositions had a profound influence on the Oriya literature composed after the *Vaiṣṇava* age. According to *Vāmana*, the Sanskrit theorist on Poetics (C 8th A.D.), "the soul of poetry is style (*Rītirātmā Kāvyasya*), which is a specified arrangement of words, the term specified referring to distinction according to the qualities possessed which are the cause of charm in poetry, while the figures are ranged as things which add to the charm".[1] This *Rīti* school in Sanskrit literature provided the inspiration for the development of *Rīti* school also in Oriya literature. Other Sanskrit compositions, e.g., *Bāṇa's Kādambarī* which is a perfect demonstration of the *Rīti* school of Poetics also went in support of it. To quote Prof. Weber "Bāṇa's style is an Indian wood, where progress is impossible through the under-growth until the traveller cuts out a path for himself and where even he is confronted by malicious wild beasts in the form of unknown words to terrify him".

"*Gītagovinda* composed by Śrī *Jayadeva* (C 12th A.D.) helped the *Vaiṣṇava age* to drift into an age of composition abounding in embellishments (*Alaṅkāras*). This age is known as *Rīti* age".[2] "*Jayadeva's* work is a masterpiece, and it surpasses in its completeness of effect any other Indian poem. It has all the perfections of the miniature word-pictures which are so common in Sanskrit poetry, with the beauty which arises, as Aristotle assents from magnitude and arrangement".[3]

The fancy, the jugglery of words, "the art of wedding sound and meaning is carried out with such success in the case

1. A history of Sanskrit Literature by Keith, p. 381.
2. Oriya Sahityara Itihāsa by Pandit Suryanarayana Dash, Part-I, p. 495.
3. A History of Sanskrit Literature by Keith, p. 194.

of *Gītagovinda* that it cannot fail to be appreciated even by ears far less sensitive than those of Indian writers on poetics".[1]

Hence in Oriya literature, this *Vaiṣṇava* age of the '*Pañchasakhā*' turned its flow to the *Rīti* age. But in spite of gorgeous embellishments, *Dhvani* and the use of Prosody in this age, the thought-process of the *Vaiṣṇava* age began to continue. In the *Vaiṣṇava* age, we do not find the compositions of any woman-poet other than *Mādhavī Dāsī*. It seems *Bṛindāvatī Dāsī* is the foremost poetess, worthy of being mentioned, after *Mādhavī Dāsī*. She was both a poetess and a scholar; hence her place in the literary field was quite high. Besides, she was born in a family of *Litterateurs* and being the mother and grandmother of such *Litterateurs* her place is still higher".[2]

The compositions of *Upendra Bhañja*, *Abhimanyu Sāmanasiṁhāra* and others, which were full of wonderful embellishments and prosody, lighted the firmament of Orissa. Hence it is strange that the poetic compositions full of religious matters composed by *Vaiṣṇavī Bṛindāvatī Dāsī* belonging to the *Vraja Cult* could be liked immensely. But it seems the *Kāvya* composed in the refined language, and the earnest appeal of a pious devotee were accepted by the lovers of poetry and the *Vaiṣṇavas* simultaneously as Kāvya and Scripture.[3]

It is a matter of surprise that the "*Pūrṇatama Chandrodaya Kāvya*" of *Bṛindāvatī Dāsī* was free from all kinds of complications of the *Rīti Age*, though the *Rīti* school held its full sway during that period.

Bṛindāvatī Dāsī :

Bṛindāvatī Dāsī was born in the village of *Malipaḍā* in the district of Purī. This village is situated sixteen miles away from the town of Purī. *Bṛindāvatī* married in a renowned *Karaṇa* family. Her husband's name was *Chandraśekhara Mahāpātra*. The family of *Chandraśekhara*, for generations

1. A history of Sanskrit Literature by A.B. Keith, p. 195.
2. Oriya Sahityara Itihāsa, Part II, by Pandit Suryanarayana Dash, p. 470.
3. Ibid.

together were followers of the *Brajavaiṣṇava* School. As the family members of *Chandraśekhara* were *'Vaiṣṇavas'* they adopted the title of *'Dāsa'* instead of *Mahāpātra.*

The poetesses, during the reign of the feudal chief *Divyasiṁha Deva* of Khurdā (13th Aṅka) and the end of C 17th A.D. composed the Kāvya "*Pūrṇatama Chandrodaya*". By that time her husband Chandraśekhara had already composed the Kāvya known as '*Śrīkṛiṣṇachandra-tattva*', her son Bhīma Dāsa '*Bhaktiratnāvalī*' and her grandson '*Upāsanāchandrodaya*'. Though Chandraśekhara's family members were the devotees of *Kṛiṣṇa* from generation to generation, still they were householders and worshipped *Kṛiṣṇa* in their houses. Consequently they took up their pens to eulogise the merits of the god and composed poetry according to their individual capacities. In the *Kāvya*, the poet has admitted of taking help from her husband. Once she asked her husband the question :—*Gopa*, *Mathurā* and *Dvārakā*—in these three places—which is *Pūrṇatama*, which is *Pūrṇatara*, and which is *Pūrṇa*?

"*Nitya golaka pūrṇatama, aṭanti puruṣa uttama,*
Prabhu rahiṇa martyapura, lilā je kale tinithara,
A tinitharu, keuthare pūrṇatamatā prakāśile,
Rahiṇa kebaṇa hi deśe, ābara kebaṇa bayase.

(*Pūrṇatama Chandrodaya—Dvitīya Adhyāya*)

Puruṣottama is eternal and full like the earth. God having stayed on earth, worked in three places. From amongst the three places, where did he manifest his fullest form ? In which country ? And in what age?

As an answer to this question, her husband explained to her the deeds of *Śṛīkṛiṣṇa* in his *Pūrṇatamatā*. This knowledge was definitely higher than any type of education imparted in any one of the regular schools. In his opinion *Dvārakālīlā* was full (*Pūrṇa*), *Mathurālīlā* fuller (*Pūrṇatara*) and *Gopa līlā*—fullest. As *Gopalīlā* is called *Pūrṇatama*, Śrīkṛiṣṇa is said to be *Puruṣottama* there. All these intricate matters of discourse have been placed together and the *Kāvya* named *Pūrṇatamachandro-*

daya has been composed by *Bṛindāvatī Dāsī.*

In the first Chapter, the poetess has used *Śabdālaṅkāra* and other metaphors to eulogise Kṛiṣṇa. But afterwards, taking into account the fact that the gorgeous dress of Śrīkṛiṣṇa was inimitable she has not used any *Upamā.*

> *Krīdi asama priya beni, Śri aṅga sobhā beṇudhvani*
> *A ādi guṇe brundābane, hele nuhanti āna sthāne*
> *Eṇu Śri brundābane, pūrṇatama bolanti nandanane*
>
> (*Pūrṇatama Chandrodaya—Dvitīya Adhyāya*)
>
> Our two favourites played at Bṛindāban with a harp to decorate the beauty of his (Śṛīkṛiṣṇa's) body ; so His fullest manifestation is at Bṛindāban ; so say the descendants of Nanda.

But on account of the needs of composing *Kāvyas*, the poetess has used *Mādhūrya Alaṅkāra.* For this purpose, she has used many quotations from Sanskrit works.

Niśaṅka Rāya Rāṇī :

Gradually the idea of harnessing religion into every branch of society and hence making all the compositions subserve a higher purpose attaining their fullest structure died out and at this juncture was born Niśaṅka Rāya Rāṇī in the house of Thāṭarāja Bāsudeva, in south Ganjam. In 1788 A.D. she married Śrī *Gaurchandra Niśaṅka Rāya,* the son of Śrī Rāmachandra Deva, member of a small feudal state of that district. After her marriage she found her husband indulging in wine and women. Hence she turned her mind to writing poetry. Afterwards she became widowed and returning to the house of her father, composed '*Padmāvatī Abhilāṣa*' under his patronage.

Niśaṅka Rāya Rāṇī expresses her remorse as she was not able to study under any regular education curriculum. Without worshipping the presiding Deity of her family, she worshipped the goddess *Sarasvatī.* Therefore, the day of *Śrīpañchamī* was regarded as very much auspicious by her.

Consequently, the hero of her *Kāvya* was Madhu and the heroine Padmāvatī were born on the *Śrīpañchamī* day. Along with the main story of the poem, the writer has intermingled some traditional stories of Orissa, which has gone far in adding to the beauty of the poem. Though *Padmāvatī Abhilāṣa* is not an imitation of the *Lāvaṇyavatī* of *Upendra Bhañja*, the writer has been profoundly influenced by Bhañja's description of subject matter and description of natural beauty. Such similarity, found in the description of the pleasure-lake is as follows:

Se narabara sarobara buli dekhanti śobhā
Sphatika pābachha bakulamule hoile ubhā
Nīla śāḍhi, raṅga dhaḍi je hansābali śobhana
Mahi mahilā bistārilā prāye diśe rañjana.
Padma-kumuda kokanadaṇkara subāsa gheni
Bhramare bhramare bhramanti kari haraṣa dhvani
Dīpadandī mandi sundara sārasa chakrabāka
Hansamarāli saṇge gheni karuchhanti dāhuka.

(Padmāvatī Abhilāṣa)

That king, going round the lakes, saw the beauty. Near the *Bakula* tree, where there were crystal-clear steps, he stood. This lake, like a blue *saree*, where the swans served as border, spread over the ladylike Mother-earth.

In taking the fragrance of the lotus, lily and the red-lotus, the bees move about humming joyfully. The beautiful *Sārasas*, *Chakravakas*, *Swans*, *Marālas* and *Dāhukas* are roaming about in the beautiful lake.

Ki nīla śāḍhi hansābali raṇgadhaḍi hoichhi
Abanī banitā bistāre kibā kiṇibā ichhi.
Pābachha svachha sphatikare nīratīra pratīta
Subeśī paraśa bhābi ki tahiñ tribeṇī khyāta.
Dīpadandī heri marālapanti dei bhauñrī
Baḍa baḍa bhiki beḍhi ki śobhā pūrṇa chouñri.

(Lāvaṇyavatī)

The blue *saree* with swans as the border is spread by

the ladylike Mother-earth (on her body) with a desire to display. The crystal-clear steps coming in contact with the water at the bank remind us of the beauty of a beautiful damsel of Triveṇī. The *Marālas* whirl about in the lake and being surrounded by *Bhākura* fish, they imitate the beauty of a fullfledged chowrie.

IV
THE MODERN AGE

"Old order changeth yielding place to new."

In the words of Joseph Wood Krutch—"All ages are changing ages, but during the second half of the nineteenth century many people were convinced that theirs' was such in a very special sense. They both believed and hoped that they were making a very radical break with the past, and they looked forward to a future really discontinuous with it. Some of them spoke of 'tradition' as almost wholly bad. Something, they thought, was at last setting men free, and they tended to think of only two epochs in man's history, the Past and that Future of which they were seeing the dawn."

At such a juncture in the field of Oriya compositions, three contemporaneous stalwarts were born namely, Fakirmohan Senapati, Radhanath Rai and Madhusudan Rao. All the three of them strove to introduce revolutionary concepts in establishing a rational harmony for accepting the new values and norms of life in place of the traditional ones through the medium of two most important fields of human concern—prose and poetry.

Fakirmohan Senapati (1843-1918) is said to be the pioneer in the field of modern Oriya literature. He fought against the baselessness of the view then propounded that 'Oriya is not an independent language' and was brave enough to establish the originality of Oriya language and literature. On account of his multiple compositions in the various fields of literature he was honoured with the title of "Vyāsa Kavi."

"Till the other day like the *Sāralā Age*, the Jagannāth Age and the Upendra Age, the modern age was known as Rādhānāth Age. This was, perhaps, the result of the mysterious influence which the poetry of a poet casts on the minds of the people in general. Up till now no branch of literature has been able to cast such influence on the minds of people. Hence it was natural to name this age, in accordance with the age of the poet. But the way in which modern research in Oriya literature has placed the current of events during the last sixty years, pointing to a changed value of literary merit, lead the intellectuals to opine that his age should be named by the name of the *Litterateur* Fakirmohan Senapati".[1]

"Some people, however, honour poet Rādhānāth Ray (1848-1908) as the founder of the Modern Age and hence they name Modern Age as '*Rādhānāth Age*'. Changing the old way of literary compositions as a gifted poet, creating the new taste according to age, and the literary style of poetry which he gave birth to, have influenced many of the later poets. His contribution towards Oriya literature is enormous. He has composed many a highclass poetry. Though the poet of Modern Age, he has not cast off the old style nor has he overlooked the current traditional stories though he has adopted many western stories into his compositions. Rather, a well-balanced communion between the old and new traditional stories of the east and the west is to be noticed in his writings".[2]

During this period also (1853-1912) "the devotee poet Madhusudan Rao had already prepared the ground-work of Oriya literature for the healthy growth of powerful literature. The new religious thought, the special way of presentation and taste, have regulated to a great extent the inner nature of Modern Oriya Literature".[3]

These three stalwarts of Oriya literature were bound by the thread of personal friendship and are said to have passed many a mellow summer evening arguing and discussing on topics pertaining to literature, seated on the embankments of the shady pools. This goes to a large extent in presenting a common tie between their individual literary compositions. For the first time in the range of literary history, they made Orissa known to its sister-states and the outside world also. This effective group of trio had been busy stressing the importance of the continuity of tradition rather than the reality of the chasm between the past and the future. They accepted a sort of first liberating principle, along with the fundamental resources to be the

1. Oriya Sahityara Itihāsa by Dr. Mayadhara Mansinha, p. 256. (Trans. by me)
2. Oriya Jati O Radhanath by Sri Purnachandra Rout, 'Kshaṇika'—Radhanath Viśeṣāṅka, 1969. (Trans. by me)
3. Oriya Sahityara Itihāsa by Dr. Mayadhara Mansinha, p. 314. (Trans. by me)

spirit of modern Oriya literature. The standards of modern Oriya literature were proclaimed by them to be essentially different from those of the past only when they were tested by different criteria. The renowned *litterateur* Mama Warerkar spoke in support of this—"Oriya amongst all the Indian languages was pushed to the background by the preponderance of the Bengali language and literature and it was impossible to exhibit its individual merit. Among those who gave a new life to Oriya literature were the Marathi poet Madhusudan Rao, the Bengali poet Radhanath Ray, and the Oriya poet Fakirmohan Senapati".[1]

"In the trend of literature after Radhanath, Fakirmohan and Madhusudan, two other trends of literature were seen—*Satyabādī* and *Sabuja*. A total perspective of literary, political, social hopes and desires, aspirations and dreams, thoughts and imaginations, the cultural heritage and the prevailing bad condition of the period took shape in an imaginative future national life through the medium of '*Satyabādi Sāhitya*' (1910-1920). Apart from the literature of Sāralā Dāsa, nowhere is seen this life message of Oriyas depicted in its true colour".[2]

To this Satyabādi Age, belonged the friends five in number—Pandit Gopabandhu Dash, Pandit Nilakantha Dash, Pandit Godavarish Misra, Pandit Kṛipāsindhu Misra and Pandit Lingaraj Misra. They are called the 'Pañchasakhā' of the Satyabādī Age as corresponding to the Pañchasakhā of the Vaiṣṇava Age.

After the Satyabādī Age, the Sabuja Age (1921-1935) evolved out of friendship of a group of young and progressive writers known as Sabuja. "Their compositions were deeply individual and subjective in their approach. The new poets experimented with new forms and patterns corresponding to their name as Sabuja or evergreen. This age is considered to be a golden age in the development of progressive Oriya poetry".[3]

1. Jhankar, 9th year, 2nd edn. Mama Warerkar's speech delivered in Visuva Milana—Brusha, 1364. (Trans. by me)
2. Satyabādī Juga by Sri Bṛindāban Ch. Acharya, p. 95. (Trans. by me)
3. Adhunika Oriya Sahityara Bhumi O Bhumika. Adhunika Oriya Kabitare Vastavavadi Dṛiṣṭibhaṅgi—Sri Chintamani Behera, p. 28. (Trans. by me)

In the Sabuja Age are included poets such as : Sri Anandasankar Ray, Sri Sarat Chandra Mukherjee, Sri Baikunthanath Patnaik, Sri Kalindi Charan Panigrahi and Sri Harihar Māhāpātra. After those poets, some other poets of the modern age composed their poetry according to their own independent ways of thinking and individual tendencies. These poets did not belong to any particular group or class. They were rather individualistic in their outlook and expression. They are Dr. Mayadhar Mansingh, Sri Sachidananda Rout, Sri Radhamohan Gadnaik, Sri Ananta Patnaik.

Upto the Satyabādī Age, no poetess of talent came up into the sphere of literary circle. Some poets, such as the well known *litterateur* Sri Kalindi Charan Panigrahi opine that poetesses of notable calibre appeared for the first time during the Sabuja age—"If there is no restriction in name, only then Kuntala Kumari and the poetesses of the later period can be included in the Sabuja Age."[1]

The poetry which was composed by women poetesses before this age, though devoid of high literary merit, provided quite an enjoyable reading. Such poetesses are—

Sulakshaṇa Devī:

Sulakshaṇa Devī was born in the year 1820 in the feudal state of Tigiria. She married Sri Nityananda Patnaik of Dhenkanal. Among their two sons, Sri Damodar Patnaik was said to be a 'Ustad' in Odissi songs. His recitations in musical *rāgas*, produced a cumulative effect on his mother's poetic thoughts. From her early childhood, she was very religious by nature. After her widowhood at the age of fifty, she completely dedicated herself to the service of God. In order to express such religious thoughts, she composed a book called '*Pārijātamālā*'. This bunch of poetry is replete with the sentiment of '*Bhakti*'.

Suchitrā Devī :

Suchitrā Devī was born in the year 1881 in a notable Karan

1. Satyabādī—Part I, 23rd edition.

family. She married Sri Raghabananda Das of the village Kurunjipur of the Purī district. Her husband, though employed in the Government administrative service, was contributing articles to various literary journals. Under the guidance of her husband she put together the current traditional stories of Orissa and published a collection of stories. But she is mainly a poetess. In 1901 her poetic compositions entitled '*Kavitālaharī*' was published. Afterwards, six subsequent editions of this book came out. This speaks of the popularity of her composition. Her eldest daughter Devahūti Devī is also a notable writer in Oriya literature.

Annapūrṇā Devī:

Annapūrṇā Devī was born in a Karan family in the district of Ganjam in 1883. Her father's name was Govinda Patnaik and mother's name Subhadhrā. Govinda Patnaik was a middle-class man. He had practically no education. He managed his family by doing the work of a Sarbarakar. Annapūrṇā had her education in the Pāṭhśālā (village school). By the age of nine, her education was finished. After the completion of her education, she read *Oriya Bhāgavata*, *Rāmāyaṇa*, *Mahābhārata*, *Chaitanya Charitāmṛita* etc.

In the year 1900, at the age of seventeen years Annapūrṇā married Sri Ramachandra Patnaik of Puruṣottamapur in the district of Ganjam. Sri Ramachandra Patnaik was a low-paid employee in the court of the feudal king of Parlakhimundi. His wife served as giving companionship to the queen of His Highness. Though poor, this couple could visualise things much ahead of their time. Hence, through the patronage of her husband, the poetic genius of Annapūrṇā began to develop. As its first instance, she wrote certain poems full of the sentiment of 'Devotion,' welcoming the birth of the new-born baby to the queen.

The magazine 'Sahakāra' which was established for the first time by the Late Sri Lakhsminarayana Sahu, was published for sometime under the editorship of Annapūrṇā. Amongst her Kāvyas '*Padyamālā*' is famous. Part-I of this book was printed and published by Pandit Nilamani Vidyaratna for the first time in 1904. This consists of '*Prarthana*', *Go-dhana*', '*Bahuda*', '*Puspa*', '*Patipatninka Prathama*', '*Bidhatare Prathama*' and '*Jibe Daya*'. In 1905, Part-II of '*Padyamala*' was printed and published. '*Brahmaprarthana*', '*Nishihelani*', *Bṛikshamanankara shova*', '*Bhaktiprarthana*', '*Sansara-Chitra*' and '*Staba*' and other poems are found in this part. In 1907, '*Pakshighara*' and '*Bhaktiprarthana*' were printed and published. Besides this Annapūrṇā has left behind a lot of unpublished work. Putting them all together, will make a large collected work. In 1961, this poetess died at the residence of Sm. Manorama Patnaik, her eldest daughter who was then the Inspectress of Schools.

Literature after World War I:

"After the conclusion of World War I (1914-1918) a new school of thought sprang up in India. Mahatma Gandhi showed the way to non-violence. On the 24th March, 1921 Mahatma Gandhi came to Orissa. This helped Orissa in assimilating thoughts which were current on All-India level. The nationalism of Utkala Sammilani gained dimension on All-India basis. The values of this consciousness of nationalism began to be reflected in the literary compositions. Utkala Sammilani (1903), Bengal-partition (1905), division of Bihar and Orissa as separate provinces (1936) roused a stir in the minds of the intelligentsia class. Contemporaneously, the women of Orissa tried to free themselves from the heavy tie of social customs and traditional rules and regulations. On account of the advent of the *Brahmo-Samaj* in Orissa, the fight for the emancipation of women broadened its scope. Respect and regard for women began to be valued in society. The agitation for women's emancipation began to influence the thought-process of the *Sabuja* poets."[1]

The daughters of Sri Biswanath Kar, the founder of the Brahmo Samaj of Orissa—Narmada, Prativa, Suprava and Shailabala (adopted daughter of Utkala Gouraba Madhusudan Das) were highly educated in the western system of education

1 Adhunika Oriya Sahityara Bhumi O Bhumika—Sabuja Kavitara Dhara by Raghabananda Naik—p. 99. (Trans. by me)

according to the standard of that age. These women became the leaders of women-emancipation movement. They were influenced by such Western scholars and their philosophy as Carlyle and Emerson. Hence taking in the good ideas from the West, these educated women translated some worthy literature of the West and wrote out some original essays, which they published in different magazines. It is said—"Once Emerson, who had an eastern trend of thinking, went to see Carlyle and Carlyle presented him the Gīta, and that little book is responsible for the Concord movement."[1]

During the period concerned the most disquieting feature of the women in Orissa was the almost impenetrable barrier raised between them and their male partners due to the lack of education amongst the general mass of women. On account of this handicap, bright young Oriyas returning from England, highly qualified as I.C.S. officers or bar-at-law's chose to marry non-Oriya girls, who were by that time more enlightened in the Western way of education. The duty of bringing the light of education to the huge illiterate and uneducated mass of women in Orissa, fell into the hands of these advanced ladies of the Bramho Samaj. The women in general did not have a knowledge of English. As the first step towards making them familiar with the Western line of thought, the worth-while works of Western literature were translated into Oriya with great pains by these volunteering ladies enthused with a spirit of self-sacrifice and dedication. "Smt. Narmada Kar translated the works of Tolstoy and published them under the caption—'*Bandi*', '*Bibadabhanjana*', '*Parinama*', '*Dandabidhana*', '*Trusna*', *Kuhuka*' and '*Santi*' etc."[2]

Afterwards, these works were collected and published in the form of a book called '*Bideshi*'. Smt. Prativa Devi, the sister of Narmada Devi also published '*Swapna*, (as the translation of Ivan Turgenev's 'Dream') and *Bideshi Kāvyagrantha*' as the translation of 'Peter Bell.'

Besides this, '*Purnima Rajani*' by Smt. Gopal, '*Sarama*' by Nagendrabala Saraswati, the story 'Apa' by Suprava Devi, '*Swarupa*' poem by Kokila Devi, the short story '*Deva Darsan*'

1. The Complete Works of Swami Vivekananda, Vol. IV, p. 95.
2. Utkala Sahitya, Parts 20th—25th, 1328, 1333.

by Narmada Devi and also many others were published in the Utkala Sahitya.

Reba Ray:

Reba Ray (1876—1957), the niece of poet Madhusudan, appeared as a poetess of repute in the domain of Oriya literature. She was the wife of Sri Sadhu Charan Ray, then living in Jaipur. Sadhu Charan himself was also a notable writer in the field of Oriya literature. Smt. Ray made good efforts at reforming society and raising the standard of education of women to the level of the educated community of men. She was also a pioneer in the opening of the Ravenshaw Girls' School which stands with all its old glory in the city of Cuttack near Gauri Shankar Park. In 1904 she published a collection named '*Añjali*' which is a collection of forty poems. Smt. Ray also edited a paper named '*Prabhāt*'. "The short story named '*Śakuntalā*' written by Smt. Ray seems to be the first original short story written in Oriya by women".[1]

1. Oriya Sahityara Itihāsa by Natabara Samantaray, p. 533.

V

THE EDUCATIONAL ADVANCEMENT OF WOMEN IN ORISSA

Some bold steps were taken by the ladies of the Brahmo and Christian communities for the diffusion and spread of education in Orissa amongst the illiterate mass of women.

In order to learn the advanced methods of education, in 1918, Smt. Sailabala Das, the adopted daughter of the famous barrister Madhusudan Das, sailed for England. During her stay in England, a diary under the caption '*Bilat Prabasa*,' written by her, was being published regularly in Utkala Sahitya. This provides a replica of the style of prose literature of the period—

"Then I was at Cambridge. It was winter. I could not think of as how to spend this winter. When I saw that the Sun was not visible—it was cloudy, the trees were devoid of leaves and Nature had put on the marks of sorrow, then my mind, burdened with grief at the parting from my relatives and friends, became one with the feelings of Nature. No effort could make my mind cheerful. My mind was longing to return to my own country. I was thinking if I could visualise the Sun even once in two or three days, then in the green leaves of trees on the jovial face of Nature, I could get some cheerfulness in my mind"[1].

After her return to Cuttack and settling down there permanently, she began to think of establishing a Girls' School, exclusively for the education of girls.

A Girls' School was there already in existence, where the courses of studies were fixed upto Middle Vernacular and the medium of instruction was both Bengali and Oriya. Basanti, the daughter of Bhaktakavi Madhusudhan Rao, and Nisamani, the daughter of Rai Bahadur Nandakishore Ray, passed the Middle School scholarship examination in 1886, as the first among the girl candidates. After one or two years, Reba (Reba Ray) and Basumati, the daughter of the famous lawyer Priyanath

1. **Utkala Sahitya—Falguna-Chaitra, 11th-12th Edition, Year 1317.**
(Trans—by me)

Chatterjee passed the same examination. In 1892, Avanti, another daughter of Madhusudan Rao passed out from this School. After this, the school closed down. In 1905, Smt. Reba Ray established a school for Girls at Cuttack named Model Girls' School. Smt. Ray laboured hard to develop this School by her manual labour as well as by the investment of money. A girl named Chandramukhi Sarangi passed out from this school in the entrance examination. She was a converted Christian. Smt. Ray brought some Brahmo teachers and lady teachers for teaching, in this school.

Smt. Shailabala Das in collaboration with Smt. Reba Ray, converted this Model Girls' School into Ravenshaw Girls' School. This was the first permanent step taken towards the advancement of women's education in Orissa. Later on, this private school was taken over by the Government of Orissa and then Intermediate classes in Arts were started.[1]

To-day we have Shailabala Women's College at Cuttack, one of the premier Women's Colleges of the State. It is a separate and full-fledged college with facilities of Science, Arts and Honours teaching curriculums.

The Ravenshaw Girls' School stands as it was in its old place near the Gauri Shankar Park, Cuttack, with its dilapidated old building standing as a remembrancer of the hoary past. I am proud of having both the Ravenshaw Girls' School and the Shailabala Women's College as my '*Alma Mater*' with such teachers as Smt. Prativa and Smt. Suprava Kar and lecturers as Miss. Chanda, Miss Hazra and Miss Khan (at present Mrs. Sinha) and as Headmistress-cum Principal, Miss Nayak, a strict disciplinarian.

I had the pleasure of serving under Mrs. Sinha for a few months when she was the Principal of the Shailabala Women's College.

Those dedicated teachers made us study, act in dramas, write essays, take part in debates and play in the bright sunlit fields. The melodious piano recitals played by our esteemed teacher Miss Khan (now Mrs. Sinha) still haunt our memories.

Mixed with this were the angry reproaches of those

1. **Bhaktakavi Madhusudan Rao O Utkale Navayug by Smt. Avanti Devi.**

teachers whenever we were at fault, and also their affectionate pats when anything good was noticed. In short, dynamism was enthused into our adolescent lives accompanied by the usual joys and tears and we sucked in greedily whatever was worthy of being consumed in life.

With grateful obeisance I bow down to those teachers, some of them living and some dead. May my prayers touch their souls, which used to pour forth blessing, making me what I am today.

Education of women in India, nay in Orissa, has taken rapid strides in recent times. Sophisticated women are no more the butts of satire in contrast to its fascination in earlier days. The rapid and radical changes that are taking place in a woman's life have resulted in the change of values in life.

The old mothers-in-law are being pushed to the background whereas the newly married daughters-in-law have come up to hold their sway in all house-hold matters. This pattern is being imitated by the East from the West. To quote Swami Vivekananda—"In the West, the woman is wife. The idea of womanhood is concentrated as the wife. To the ordinary man in India, the whole force of womanhood is concentrated in motherhood. In the Western home the wife rules, in the Indian houses the mother rules."[1]

The modern women have no faith in the ancient ideals set before them by Scriptures and mythologies. They are more concerned about the present comforts of living and enjoyment of life, rather than the thought of the deliverance of their souls in after-life. Hence refrigerators, air-conditioners and gadgets of all kinds have an importance added to that of the fondness of jewelry. Women no longer want to remain confined to the four-walls of their houses and therefore are marching on in equal strides with their male partners.

The older generation is silently and unhappily watching the changes but is too feeble-minded to protest. The modern woman is marching ahead with very little hindrance to retard her progress. Whether this will lead her to heaven or to hell is another question.

1. The Complete Works of Swami Vivekananda, Vol. VIII, p. 57.

Kuntalakumari Sabat :

Kuntalakumari Sabat was the first Oriya lady to serve the country as a ladydoctor. Side by side with her career as a lady doctor, she carried on her literary pursuits and established herself as a worthy writer in the realm of Oriya literature.

"In the year 1900, in a stormy night, was born Kuntalakumari Sabat. Like a storm also, her life was extinguished in 1938, at an early age of thirty-eight only. The story of Kuntalakumari, which brought about a stir in the Oriya literary field, has now been turned into a myth."[1]

Born in a family of a Christian father, named Daniel Sabat, she spent her childhood and adolescent days with her father in connection with his job in the distant land of Burma. On her return from Burma, she joined the then Medical School and took the teachers and her class-mates by surprise by standing first in each of the examinations. Then she gave up her Christianity and reconverting herself into Hinduism by the rules of Arya Samaj, married Krishnaprasad Brahmachari at Delhi. After her marriage, she settled down at Delhi and at a time when her medical profession and literary career were at the pinnacle of glory, she suddenly passed away from this world.[2]

"Most of the compositions of Kuntala kumari are centred around God. Though she was a Christian lady, she studied the Bhagavad Gītā, Upaniṣad and the Kāvyas of Gauḍīya Vaiṣṇava literature and was deeply influenced by them. By the composition of *Tārā Prati*, a nationalistic poem, Kuntalakumari started her literary career, which has taken shape into a fullfledged development in '*Sphuliṅga*' and *Āhvāna*'. Amongst her Kāvyas, *Añjali*, *Archanā*, *Sphuliṅga* and *Prema Chintāmaṇi* are the chief ones. In *Prema Chintāmaṇi* Kāvya, her love of God, has attained a glorious height. In the poems of Kuntalakumari, God is not bound by any religion. He resides in and out of every religion. Nobody can find Him in his own heart though He dwells

1. Oriya Sahityara Itihāsa, Dr. Mayadhara Mansinha, p. 311.
2. Ibid.

closely in every heart".[1]

Hence the poetess writes—

Kruṣṇa kahi kehi kare ārādhanā,
Christạ kahi kehi karuchhi bandanā.

(Pūjāpaddhati—Añjali—Kuntalakumari Granthamālā, Part-I, Page-30)

Some worship God in the name of Kṛiṣṇa, some worship in the name of Christ, all are the same, all are devotion, all are true, nothing is false.

Kuntalakumari was also a poetess of Nature. She describes the natural beauties in communion with the human emotions bringing out in the long run a philosophical moral out of their comparison. In her poem entitled *Śephāli Prati*, she writes—

Shephāli !

Toha pari ksudra muhiñ, toha pari ksaṇika,
Hase, bāse, rase mātra phutiachhi ghaḍika.
Mātire miśibu tuhi, mātire miśibi muhiñ,
Tathāpi mo ātmāphula na jibare mauli,
Teṇu āśā bahi dina kāte gangaśeuli.

× × ×

Śeṣa gati nuhe mora mrutyu keuñ kālare,
Maribāku phuti achhi bhavataru dālare.
Achhi ramya upabana jahiñ phuti chiradīna
Ananta amruta prema sudhāmaya subāse
Mohibi mo prāṇapriya devatāṇku ullāse.[2]

Śephāli !

I am small and transitory like you,
I have blossomed only for a moment with

1. Kuntalakumari Granthamala, Part I, 'Preface'.
2. Shephāli Prati—'Uchhvāsa' Kuntalakumari Granthamala, Part-1, p. 72.

Smile, fragrance and sweet juice.
You will crush yourself unto the earth,
I will also crush myself unto the earth,
Still my flower-like Soul will not fade,
Hence, Oh: Gaṅgaśeuli! I spend my days with hope.
My ultimate aim is not death at any time,
I have not blossomed in the branch of the world-tree in order to perish.
There is a certain pleasure-garden, where blossoming for ever,
I will appease my favourite God with my fragrance of eternal and everlasting love.'

The first thing perhaps which strikes a reader of Kuntalakumari's poems, is the fundamental religious basis of the entire literature. This philosophical attitude has been supported by a general moral purpose to encourage virtue and condemn vice and sin. Her poems tend to be optimistic, rather than being pessimistic. The fiery constructions in order to enthuse the spirit of 'Awake! Arise' into the hearts of the then demoralised women of Orissa, the idealistic representation, exquisite lyricism and lofty morals conveyed by the poetry of Kuntalakumari, made her an eminent poetess of India. Placed in the background of romantic setting, her poems gave the fullest altitude to imagination.

The lives of women in Orissa were, at that time, miserable, being oppressed by social law and order. They used to live a hell of living, being guided by the wheel of illiteracy, superstition and above all the lack of a firm will to resist all injustice advanced towards them. Kuntalakumari was the first one to enkindle the ray of hope in their hearts and make them strong enough to fight out their rights. Her fiery calls in *Sphuliṅga* for the purpose are—

Śata taruṇa taruṇī komala antare
Deśaprema puṇya-phalgu bahe nirantare
Lāje luchi rahichhanti nibāse,
Deśapremī karmavīra nairāśya udāse.

Jāo tebe go śphuliṇga ksudra agnikaṇā,
Āṇa jībane ananta ānanda preraṇā,

Bahu pachhe jhañjā ghora, bhīma prabhañjana
Na libhu tohara dīpta hasita ānana.
Jāla prati prāṇe deśa-prema dīpa
Etiki āśīsa heu viśva-adhīpa.

In the soft hearts of hundreds of young boys and girls, the Phalgu-like river of patriotism flows everlastingly. But out of shyness and despair such heroes have hidden themselves in their houses.

Then you small spark of fire go and bring into life, the eternal joy of inspiration.

Let fierce storms and wind blow—
Let not your bright and smiling face be extinguished.
You light in every heart the flame of patriotism.
You the Lord of the Universe, bestow on me this much of blessing.

Against all obstacles she sent out courageous soldiers to fight, inspiring them with speeches full of youth and vigour.

Kipaiñ kāndibi ākule jananī
Kari na pārili śevā go,
Kipaiñ nindibi karamaku mora
Hoibi muñ jāhā hebā go.
Uṇā nuheṇ mora śakati bhakati
To lāgi bandhana se mora mukati,
Basi to payare pūjibi ādare
Bahibi jā bahi nevā go.
Para pīḍā dukha bahibi muñ śire
Sahibi griṣama baraṣā sisire
Poḍu prāṇa mora āsu dukha ghora
Debi jagate jā debā go.[1]

Why shall I cry piteously mother, because I could not serve you, why should I blame my fate ? I will be what I am destined to be.

1. Archana—Kuntalakumari Granthamala, Part I, p. 110.

My strength and devotion are not less important. The bondage for your sake is my emancipation.

I will sit down at your feet and worship you, and I will carry whatever I have to shoulder.

I will carry on my head the sorrow of the sufferings of others bearing the sun, the rain and the winter.

Let my life be burnt, let huge catastrophies fall on me. I will give unto the world, whatever I have to spare.

"After Fakirmohan, Kuntalakumari was the first one to discover the noble hearts dwelling in the neglected, tortured and down-trodden characters of society. Her contributions to novels are milestones in the history of novel in Oriya literature. She is the first woman novelist in the field of Oriya literature. Hence her historical importance in this respect is not less".[1]

"All the novels of Kuntalakumari are social novels—*Bhrānti*, *Naotuṇdi*, *Kālibohu*, *Paraśamani*, *Raghuarakṣita* etc. exhibit the voice of protest raised by the author against social injustice and torture. In all the novels Kuntalakumari has paid great tributes to Orissa and the Oriyas. She has tried also to eulogise the Oriya race in the far off land of Burma and the city of Calcutta. As soon as she gets a little of opportunity, she showers praises through the characters of the Oriya country and race, their behaviour, and their movements created by her, e.g.—the characters of 'Raghuarakṣita', Naresh and Jyotiṣa reveal the truth—"Who else cooks food better than Oriya girls? Really brother, the cakes (Maṇḍā) you prepare, the crushed flattened rice (Churā-ghaṣā) and the baked cakes (Poḍa-pīthā) which I ate at Puri are superb; can cakes and biscuits match with them?' The Brahmin girls in Oriya families cook very well and are fond of guests. I have not seen it elsewhere—that place is the playground of Lord Jagannāth—the place of Mahaprasād. Goddess Lakṣmī herself cooks there".[2]

Kuntalakumari had a mind of her own. Her literary compositions also reflected the same viewpoint of life. She did

1. Kavi O Kavita—Dr. Mayadhar Mansinha, p. 130-132.
2. Raghuarakṣita, p. 200 and Oriya Sahityara Bhumika, p. 181.

not appreciate the line of stereotyped literary compositions. She spoke on the occasion of an All-Orissa literary conference, "the modern world does not appreciate the literature where there are only rhyming lines, or at best a description of love or erotic sentiments, but no treasure acquired out of deep thought and perseverance. When the country is writhing in revolutionary thoughts, economic distress, agitations of labourers, and the political life is cloudy, who will care for us if we go on composing romantic ballads? The literature pertaining to the benefit of our country and the individuals has yet to take its birth."

In her personal life, Kuntalakumari was an artist, religious devotee, and national leader. In her compositions, we find, the dream of a lover, the spirit of a soldier, the religious thoughts of a devotee and the zeal of a revolutionary. Her literary compositions did not remain confined to the boundary of Oriya literature only. While at Delhi, she composed a collection of lyrics in Hindi known as 'Banamālā'. She also took up the responsibility of editing 'Mahāvīra Jībana' and 'Nārī Bhāratī.' By this, she also became established in the domain of Hindi literature. She was felicitated by the Muktimandap Sabhā for her literary achievements and 'Mahilā-bandhu-Samiti' conferred on her the title of 'Utkala Bhāratī.'

In 1940, under the auspices of Nabayuga Sāhitya Saṁsad, a souvenir of Kuntalakumari was published under the editorship of poet Radhamohan Garnaik. A collection of the compositions of Kuntalakumari has been published under the caption of 'Kuntalakumari Granthamala' by Dr. Kunjabehari Dash. This is a valuable contribution to the field of Oriya literature.

Aparna Devi :

After Utkalbhāratī Kuntalakumari, 'Kavitākalpalatā' Aparna Devi composed a kāvya known as *Indumatī*. Though she was not as scholarly or talented as Kuntalakumari Sabat, she was a powerful writer. In the domain of Oriya literature,

2 Sahakara, Phalguna 1340, 11th Number.

Indumatī Kāvya is well established. The poetess writes in the Preface of the Kāvya—

"I have never studied anything other than in a primary school. I passed my days in performing household duties. I get little of leisure. I cannot get a good book to read on account of poverty, but I do not know why I like to compose poetry. Prompted by such a desire, I wrote this book."

'Indumatī kāvya' is written in the pattern of Sanskrit kāvyas. In very simple language, the poet has delineated the subtle thoughts of a woman's heart.

Jāhāṭhāre priti huai jāhāra
kāyamanovākyaprāṇe
Tāhāṭhāre dhāli dia sabu sneha
pratidāna se na jāṇe.[1]

When affection develops for a particular person, the whole of the body, mind and words are concentrated on him—all affectionate actions are showered on him without a desire for return.

Again the sense of duty of a woman :—

Nārīra kartavye Vasumatī prāye
samasta kaṣaṇa sahi,
Puruṣa mangala kārye hebā bratī
chhāya pari pāśe rahi.[2]

It is the duty of a woman to bear all pains like Mother Earth and work for the good of the menfolk moving like shadows with them.

Besides following the footsteps of the original 'Daśakumāracharitam', written by Daṇḍī in Sanskrit, she wrote *Daśakumāra charita* and *Daśakumarī charita* in Oriya prose. On account of the easy flowing style and artistic descriptions, these works have been very much appreciated by the public. Besides this, she has composed '*Chintā*', '*Kavitāñjali*,' '*Bāramāsī*,' and the like. Her short story named '*Kañchanamālā*' and the

1. Indumati—III. p. 55.
2. Ibid.

poems entitled '*Āṣāḍha*' and '*Bhādrava*' were published in the journal of Utkala Sāhitya.[1]

At this period, the creative talents of Oriya writers began to dwindle. The novelists and poets of the 19th century such as Fakirmohan, Madhusudan and Radhanath were no more in this world. The Satyabādī group which took the lead in the composition of Oriya literature since 1910, took to politics and were put in jail. Politics dominated the field of Orissa rather than literature. The political and national consciousness of Orissa awakened into a mass movement. Smt. Rama Devi, Smt. Malati Chowdhury, Smt. Sarala Devi and the like freed themselves from the age-old restriction of 'purdah' and offered themselves at the altar of freedom movement.

These married Hindu women created a landmark in the history of Orissa by coming out to public platform to take leading part in the struggle for freedom.

Smt. Sarala was not satisfied by merely joining the National Congress as a freedom fighter, but she also took to pen to advertise her viewpoints as she believed in the maxim 'Pen is mightier than sword'. After this two other sisters of Sarala Devi, Smt. Nirmala Devi and Smt. Haripriya Devi appeared in the literary sphere of Orissa. On account of this march of women to the public platform both on the political, social and literary fields, and maintaining side by side a well-balanced family life at home, made the menfolk revise their attitude, as regards the position and status of women in society. This led to the exposure of barbarism, directed against the womenfolk by the hostile classes.

To-day India has advanced; qualified ladies are allowed to occupy high posts in the various departments of services. There is no sexbar in such appointments. To crown all achievements of women, Mrs. Indira Gandhi occupies one of the topmost positions in our country as the Prime minister of the Republic of India. Paradoxically, she is to-day the most loved and at the same time the most criticised woman in our country. We feel to-day that women have again returned

1. Utkala Sahitya, Part-15, 1318, 19 year.

to the ancient Vedic age, when the Vedic seers used to sing—

> *Samānī va ākūtiḥ samānā hṛdayāni vaḥ,*
> *Samānamastu vo mano yathā vaḥ susahāsati.*

(Irrespective of caste, creed and sex) let our prayers be the same, let our hearts be the same, let our minds be the same, so that all of us can get together.

Sri Basudev Kanungo was the father of Sarala Devi and Nirmala Devi, who were born in a respectable Karan family in the village Narilo of Cuttack district. According to the convention of those days, both the sisters were married at an early age, for which reason they could not progress very much in the normal curriculum of school or college education. But through their individual efforts, they studied literature and religious scriptures at home.

Now we have arrived at the door-steps of the contemporary field of literature in Orissa, as such writers are still living.

Some critics are of opinion that review of contemporary literature is not worth having since such criticisms cannot be objective. On account of the personal acquaintance and relationship with the living *litterateurs*, the real perspective of such criticism tends to be biased, The other reason is that a considerable amount of lapse of time is required for a published book to be judged and evaluated.

But against this opinion, arguments have been put in. However much a scholar may be learned or far-sighted, it is not possible for him to pass a final verdict or evaluate any work *ad finem* since in consideration of the different periods, environments and outlooks, each composition can be interpreted in a different way."[1]

Moreover, the criticism on contemporary literature makes the writer conscious of his or her own limitations, feelings or overestimation—whatever it may be. This makes the writer's path easy to make up for the defects.

1. Samakalina Rachana O Sahitya Gobesana, by Dr. Narendranath. Misra—Jhankar, 13th Year, 4th November, Karkata, 1368. (Trans. by me)

But such criticism should always be constructive, not destructive. For a criticism where "personal attacks, looking down upon others, predominate, cannot come up to a high order, for personal ego is revealed there in all its baseness. The nature of the personal ego is such that it does not admit of reconciliation. Hence, such personal ego of one person cannot suppress the personal ego of another person. Consequently, both the egos collide with each other and literary criticism becomes a platform for angry and loud reproaches and rebukes. Thus good taste should be taken recourse to, in the field of literary criticism. This sense of values and proportion makes the literary criticism dignified. The individual and the society which can channelize such pervertive criticisms can claim to be cultured and civilised and well-balanced".[1]

Sarala Devi :

Sarala Devi was one of the foremost soldiers amongst the Hindu Oriya women in the fight for freedom. She took active part in the Lavaṇa Satyāgraha (Salt-campaign) or 'passive resistance' in connection with the manufacture of salt. She was imprisoned many a time for such activities. Till now she puts on homespun (Khaddar) clothes. '*Kavi Gopālakriṣṇa-prativā*' and '*Śārala Mahābhāratare Nārī Charitra*' were two of her critical essays published in the Journal *Utkala Sāhitya*.[2]

After the formation of the Sabuja Sāhitya Samiti (1921-1935), a novel named *Bāsantī* was published in collaboration with a number of writers in the pattern of the *Barowari* novel of the Bengali literature. The chapter written in this book by Smt. Sarala Devi, proves her literary merit. In '*Kuntalakumārī Kaviprativā*' she has analysed the talent of poetess Kuntala-kumārī. Her book entitled '*Rāya Rāmānanda*' is a work of merit throwing light on Orissan Vaiṣṇavism. A collection of one-act plays named '*Panchapradeepa*' has also been published. In the year 1969, she has been honoured by the Orissa Sahitya Academy for her literary achievements. Some other literary organisations have also similarly honoured her.

1. **Editorial Jhankar, 5th Number, Simha, 1358,**
2. **Utkala Sahitya—14th Number, year 1348.**

Nirmala Devi

Like the 'Aonian' harp, the sensitive mind of this poet, vibrates in response to every sight and sound in Nature. Hence she pours forth her music in '*Dinānte*', an anthology of poems—

Vikāsichha mā go dīna a kānane
ei je ketoti phula,
Śaktī vukura muktā mohara
ki achhi tāhāra tula.
Satya sarāge karuṇā keśare
kshamā pīratira jale,
Jīhana surabhī buṇantu mahīre
tohari āsīṣa tale.

Oh ! mother ! in this poor garden, the flowers, which you have made to blossom, are the pearls and the strength of my heart. Is there anything of the like? Accompanied by truth, piety, forbearance and affection, let them distribute the fragrance of life under your blessings.

The śleṣa embellishment in this poem, implying a double meaning for her own children and also her poem is enjoyable.

The collection in '*Dinānte*' is lyric poetry in character.

Bisva bipaṇi eḍāi nimiṣe
basithili jebe sindhu kūle,
Lohita patākā urdhve uḍāi
jauthile bhānu asta chūḍe.
Jibana beuśā karigali jete
hisāba nikāśa karili tahiñ,
Lābha aṇke mo śūnya paḍichhi
bipula kshati muñ jaichhi sahi.

Supta chetanā jāgilā nimiṣe
ākula sindhu bakshe chāhiñ,
Urmi uthai tarṇi ābege
kshaṇakare puṇi milāe kāhiñ.[1]

After coming away from the shops of the world, when I sat down near the sea for a moment, the Sun was going down in the setting-mountain, unfurling the red-flag high up.
I have indulged in the bargain of life, but I have not settled my accounts as yet.
I have not gained anything as 'Profit', instead, I have suffered heavy loss.
In a flash my dormant sensitivity was awakened by observing the endless sea.
The waves rise up in a moment like a calf and also ebb out in a moment.

After this, the poetess awakes from her sweet reverie and her mature pen indulges in writing devotional poems. The collection of such poems is published in her book called 'Sīmānte'.

The poetess has been honoured by the Orissa Sahitya Academy in the year 1970 for her literary pursuits.

Harapriya Devi:

Smt. Harapriya is the cousin sister of Smt. Sarala Devi and Smt. Nirmala Devi. She contributed some literary compositions basing on the problems of the country and nation of that time. In her poems we get a panoramic picture of rural scenes and the sentiment of devotion. Such compositions are—'*Hemantalakṣmī*', '*Chaitrasandhyā*', '*Phāguṇarāṇī*', *Śaratpalli*' '*Āryanārī O Rāṣṭradhvaja*, etc. The Bhagavadgītā rendered by her into poem is quite enjoyable.

Bidyutprava Devi:

Immense in number are the poems of this poetess and she has also published an anthology of her poems—enormous in size. She is now considered to be an established writer in the literary field. This anthology of poems is divided into eleven parts—

(i) *Lokāyana*, (ii) *Pallīpatha*, (iii) *Sundara adharā* (iv) *Priya O Priyā* (v) *Gāthā* (vi) *Śraddhāñjali* (vii) *Khadyotikā* (viii) *Bhaktimālya* (xi) *Gadya kavitā* (x) *Jāhāku-jiye* (xi) *Kūnlu jībana*.

The well-known *Litterateur* Padmabhusan Kalindicharan Panigrahi in his Foreword to this Anthology says:—

"When we open any page of the huge Anthology of poems of Bidyutprava, the eyes are fixed in its simple language and the mellowness of Prosody devoid of artificiality of life. The poetess is blessed with the feelings which pertain to the senses and which are beyond the senses to suggest an elevated vision of life constituting the essence of poetry". (Trans. by me)

Though Bidyutprava was not highly educated, her gift for writing poetry is fully developed. Instead of gathering her knowledge of natural beauty from the scenic descriptions in books, she goes on to depict them as they were visualised by her personally. In the poem *Svāgata*, she writes—

Puṣpa taḷapa chhāḍi uthiāsa kavi
Tumaku dākuchhi nuā phaguṇara
snigdha golāpi chhabi
Dākuchhi gandha bakula champā mallī
Prabhāta aniḷe dohali dākai ballī,
Madhumālatira mañjari dāke naiñ
He nabina kavi Lekhanī ayase
Ānkī jao mora chhai.

Oh! Poet! get up from your flowery bed
You are being invited by the sweet rosy picture of the refreshing spring time.

The fragrance of *Bakula*, *Champā* and *Jasmine* are calling—the creepers are also calling you, being wafted by the morning breeze. The buds of '*Madhumālatī*' bend down to say—Oh! bewitching poet! paint my picture, please.

The abundance of Orissa's rural scenic beauty has enriched her poetry. In the poem '*Śarat*' she writes:—

Digabodhu āji śukla bouda-basanā
Katīre ābari uṣāra aruṇa raśana
Nirmala āji dharanī
Naba rūpa dhare bana bila pāṭa saranī.

Pankaja āji dekhai sūrya sapana,
Raktima ruchī dharichhi kumuda lapana
jāgrata dhara alase,
Mugdhe añaa saragara sunā kalaśe.[1]

The bride of the quarters has put on the garment of white clouds, on her loins is the red girdle of Dawn—the Lady-Earth is now very bright—the ploughed fields, ditches and roads are now putting on fresh look.

The lotus is dreaming of the Sun—the face of the lily is reddened—Lady Earth is rising up leisurely and amazingly; she gazes at the golden pitcher of the sky.

Brahmhotri Mohanti:

The poetess represents the struggles and conflicts of life in communion with Nature with her deepest convictions and sympathies. Such poems of Smt. Brahmhotri Mohanti have been published in different fortnightlies and journals. Her poem named '*Mahānagarīra Rātri*' is a bridge between the modern and ultramodern phases of poetry, tending a bit more towards ultra-modernism—

Rājapathe yānara bhairavī,
pathapārśve vipaṇīra melā

Tathāpi a bhujangara chumbanare amruta rahicchi.
Śirāpraśirāre tāra prasarichhi niśāra prabāha
Krutrima a sabhyatāra byabadhāne virahe se banchiba kipari?'

Traffic is rushing forth in the highways, shops are exhibited in the roadsides.
Yet there is nectar in the kiss of this serpent.

1. Bidyutprava Sanchayana—p. 157.
2. Mahanagarira Ratri—Jhankar, 11th year, 12th Edition, Mina 1367.

The flow of intoxication is running down through the veins, how will he live in the midst of this artificial civilization?

Tulasi Das:

Judging from the standpoint of style, language, prosody and application of sentiment (Rasa) the bunch of poems of Smt. Tulasi Das is really a bunch of Tulasi-plants. The main-stay of her poems is the realisation of the essence of religion combined with sweet rhyming verses. Hence her heart bleeds at the sight of the damage to humanity:

Lālasāra tarabārī kāte śāntī mathā
'Ism'ra darabāre dharanī je thare
Jigiṣāra jayagāne phāṭe antahpura
Mānabikatā je bandī svārtha—jaṭughare.[1]

The sword of lust cuts the throat of peace. In the court of 'ism' the earth trembles. The inner apartments re-sound with the desire to overpower. Humanity is imprisoned in the lockhouse of selfishness.

An anthology of poems named *'Kavitā Sanchayana'* has been published by the poetess. It is a collection of some of her selected poems. Out of them *'Golāpa ropaṇa'* *'Abhīṣeka'*, *Jugma-sapathā'*, *Pratyara-parājaya'*, etc. are worth mention. This writer has also published some novels, dramas, short stories and one-act plays.

Devahuti Devi :

Smt. Devahuti Devi is the daughter of the well known writer Smt. Suchitra Devi. The description of the natural beauty of Orissa by the poetess creates immense joy in the hearts of the readers. Her anthology of poems named 'Mālā' is specially enjoyable.

1. Gopabandhu Sradhasamkhya, Samaj, 1968, 'Tume jadi banchithanta sate.'

Sundaramani Patnaik:

In the poems of *Kāvyabhāratī* Sundaramani Patnaik we find mainly invocations and clarion calls for women's emancipation and progress. The procedure of the use of rhymes and juxtaposition of words illustrate her knowledge of ancient Oriya Prosody.

Such poetesses as Smt. Nalini Devi Routray, Smt. Banaja Devi, Smt. Labangalata Devi Vidusi, Smt. Kalpanakumari Devi, Smt. Kanaklata Mohapatra, Smt. Labanya Nayak, Smt. Kiranbala Tripathy, Smt. Sakuntala Panda, etc. have also made a number of contributions to the realm of poetry.

From the year 1963 onwards, Kumari Sujata has been preaching world-peace, mutual agreement and universal brotherhood through her poems. In 1970, she has been awarded an international prize for her contributions.

An anthology of poems named, 'Astajanhara Elegy' of another young poetess, named Smt. Prativa Satpathy is worth mention. The force and impact of her pen, depicting the ironies of life promise a bright future—

Samudra jātrāre kichhi hajāichha tume jeumāne
Hajāichha apaṅāra hasa kānda chhātira kalijā
O khojuchha bārambāra abisrānta dīrgha nisvāsare
Āsa jibā pañharī samudrara uttāla nīlare.

Those of you, who have lost something in your sea-voyage—those of you who have lost your joys and tears and also your heart, which you are always searching for in your endless heavy sighs, let all of us go swimming in the rising blue waves of the sea (in search of the same).

Another young writer of note comes to our memory. Shc is Smt. Bharati Singh, who has been snatched away from our midst untimely by the cruel hands of fate. Her composition—'*Sajaphula*' aud '*Gītikā*' went to a great extent in testifying her poetic merit.

1. Astajanhara Elegy by Prativa Satpathy—Samayatita, p. 49.

War Poems :

On the 20th November of the year 1962, China, all of a sudden, attacked the eastern borders of India. The war of the modern age is not through missiles only, it is also a battle of ideas and ideologies in the intellectual sphere. Hence, when India faced the real battle front, she needed a medium through which her ideas and ideologies will be preached. This patriotic call of their motherland inspired the poets of Orissa—both male and female, to publish an anthology of poems entitled '*Āgneya Śapatha*'.

Such poems inspired the women mass of Orissa to such an extent that they even parted with their much-coveted jewelery as aid to war-funds.

The poem '*Āhvāna*'—

Lunṭhana paiñ dasyura sinā
rahiachhi khāli himmat,
Se kahuñ bujhiba anya janara
śānti-sukhara kimmat ?
Āme jāṇu āma mātira mahimā bandhu !
Phiṇgichhu āme sindhu sepāre
Paradhinatara hina bojha āma skandhu

(Nalini Devi Routray)

A thief has got the courage to steal only.
How can he understand the value of the pleasure
and happiness of another man ?
Oh ! friend, we know the glory of our motherland,
We have thrown away the burden of subjugation
to the other side of the sea.

The poem '*Preraṇā*'—

Jāga dhūrjaṭi......
Jhānsi Rāṇira raṇa-biplaba
tama desha bhāle ankinta.

Tāntiatopi, Nānāsāhebara swādhīnatāmantre dikshiṭa.
Chākhi Khuntia, Surendra Sai
Chāndabibi chhabi itihāsa gāye
Jai Rajaguru, Baksi Jagabandhu, padma a desha pankara

(Sundaramani Patnaik)

Arise ! Oh Śiva !

The revolutionary war of the Rani of Jhansi is inscribed on the face of your country.

You have been initiated in the incantation of independence followed by Tantia Topi and Nanasaheb.

History eulogises Chakhi Khuntia, Surendra Sai and Chandbibi.

Victorious Rajguru, Baksi Jagabandhu are the lotus of this country.

In the poem '*Chāl, chāl, āge chāl*'—

Aji chāl, are chāl
Aṇībāku heba, nutana sūrya
Bāibāku heba, nutana tūrya
Churibāku heba, bairi sāurya
Andhara kholi, uṣā je dākuchhi purba gagana tale.
Aji chāl...chāl re chāl...
Śatru patākā dali tu chāl

[Binapani Mohanti]

March on! oh! march on!
We have to bring about the new Sun!
We have to beat the new trumpet!
We have to crush the might of the enemies!
'Dawn' is inviting you through the red eastern sky, having dispelled darkness.
March on......march on......!
March on, crushing the flag of the enemy ! !

In this anthology of poems, the contributions of Smt. Vijayini Patnaik, Smt. Sanjukta Das and Smt. Snehaprava Das are also noteworthy.

The spirit of the modern age :

The modern age consists of 'progressive literature'. Progress means to cut the ground out from under one's feet and dig a chasm into which new and current ideas can be stuffed in. Such a definition of progress implies no discontinuity with the past.

In all realms of literary compositions, three branches prevail—Poetry, Novel and Dramas. It is natural that this will also be true in case of the literature composed by women. In comparison with the well-established works of the menfolk, the allegation by some that modern poetry and novel composed by women are anaemic and trivial is not necessarily true. As a sort of natural endowment, women have the capacity for encompassing their own experiences and mirroring it with gusto and intensity. This quality is far more important than academic learning, learned discussions or the classical principles of poetic compositions, studded with examples of high intellectuality, stuffed into one's writings. Although such women writers are nimble in their compositions, still they do not fail to provide the impressiveness of a panoplied war-horse in action. Some of such writers are—

Basantakumari Patnaik :

Smt. Patnaik is one of the foremost woman-novelists of the current period, which Orissa has produced. Her novel '*Āmaḍā Bāṭa*', written a decade ago, still stands at the height of reputation as her outlook and the style of the composition of the novel are entirely original. The characters are imbibed into the atmosphere and arrangement of events of the novel. The women-characters of the novel are not the celestial beauty-nymphs like *Urvaśī*, nor are they as romantic as the delicate darlings of Upendra Bhanja. They are the most ordinary women picked up from the middle-class families. We notice here, Maya's mother as the mother of five children in a middle class family, who is crushed in between the daily domestic duties of life without a holiday—

not even a Sunday. Hence she indulges in the usual reverie of an elderly and tired woman to bring in a charming and goody-goody daughter-in-law, who not only will take up the household responsibilities, but also will nurse the mother-in-law to the best of her capacity. A philosopher once said—'Woman pays the debt of life, not only by what she does, but by what she suffers'. Our *Upaniṣads* also teach—*Tyaktena bhuñjīthā*—'Enjoy by means of renunciation only'. This is the ideology of Indian womanhood—the ancient land of Sita and Savitri.

The speciality of the novel is the portrayal of two diametrically opposite characters—Kaveri and Maya—compared and contrasted by the keenness of observation and analytical acumen of the novelist. She has not collected such characters by reading many books, analysing different theories or by divulging in imaginative explorations. She is never pedantic, nor academic, instead the depiction of her characters is intimate, profound and true to life.

Maya is trained in the 'modern' way of education. Hence her mind is analytical and free from superstitious outlook and pretensions, though rudely practical and egoistic. This is revealed through her sudden outbursts at critical junctures such as drinking the water sanctified after washing the mother-in-law's feet or hiding the pink powder in fear of its being used up by others. This radically unacademic approach to reality proves to be a guide to the reader's exploration of truth. But the same outspoken 'Maya' in her husband's family is misunderstood by her mother-in-law. The same girl, who, as a maiden was a revolutionary, as a daughter-in-law, in her attempt to consume the fire within herself, wanes herself bit by bit through self-pity. Still she preserves to the best of her efforts, a woman's virtue and character in conformity with the traditional descriptions in ancient scriptures. But Maya's sister-in-law 'Kaveri', though also educated in the 'modern' way, fails to raise herself to the height of a self-sacrificing, all-absorbing pious and gentle Hindu woman. All her pretensions to that effect only make her a laughing stock; for example, the philosophical letter written by her to Maya, when she separated herself from the family of her in-laws. She tries to conceal her offence under the garb of philosophical discourse.

The essential truth brought out of the depiction of the two characters is that modern education is not responsible for the formation of the character of a woman. It is for the women to absorb and assimilate the good out of all teachings and put them into practice in accordance with the customs, habits and rituals prevalent in one's own country.

On account of the popularity of the novel *Amāḍā Bāṭa*', it has been filmed. As a movie, it has also proved its success.

Smt. Patnaik's anthology of shortstories '*Sabhyatārā Sāja* and '*Jibanachinha*' are two valuable expositions of the various facts and struggles of life. Her '*Juarabhatta*,' '*Chorābāli*' '*Pālaṭā Dheu*,' '*Mrugatruṣṇā*' etc. depict the picture of contemporary society. The writer has written also a number of poems with soft emotions. In '*Chitānala*,' she writes—

Śāta baiśākhi jhañā āghāte
deha sinā mare thare,
Antara mora pratidina sakhi
mari jāe bāre bāre.

By the stroke of hundreds of thunder-storm,
the body dies once only—
But oh friend ! everyday my mind dies again and again.

Manorama Mohapatra :

A novel is written on the basis of some riddle or problem. The novelist creates characters of bewildering complexity in order to bring about reaction in the minds of the readers. Poetry is based on emotions of the human mind. At a certain moment, the enormous experience and emotions piled up in the subconscious mind of a poet, come out in an overwhelming flood of expressions. To quote poetess Manorama—"This poetry is not written for the sake of writing only. In the intricate parts of the hearts of the Oriya village women, the rising tide of sorrow puffs up i.e. a frothy surging up of intense heartache. Remorse, self-immolation, allegations and sensitiveness always have tidelike ebb and flow in a woman's heart. This juxtaposition, which attributes language to the silent lips of Oriya women, is not poetry, but an overwhelming flow of a disturbed and dishevelled mind." (Trans. by me)

Though this writer has written in the various branches of literature, she excels as 'Poetess'. In an anthology of poems known as '*Juāra Jeuñṭhi Uthe*', all the poems are enjoyable. Dr. Mayadhar Mansinha, an eminent *litterateur*, writes in the foreword of the book—"Many a poetess have gained fame in Oriya literature. But strange enough to say that we do not get exactly the touch of an exclusively feminine hand in the poems. They are so much well-knit and refined that we can easily replace the expert hand of any male poet as writer of such a poem. We miss the natural beauty of the uninitiated feminine hand in the depiction of various poetic colours." (Trans. by me)

\+ + +

Smt. Manorama is a modern replica of our ancient poetesses, as it were, with a feminine style of her own.

Gāān muṇda gachha hoilā pāri
galā ki sari?
Nuābohuṭira paṇata thare
Tapata lotaka niyata jhare
jharaṇā pari—[1]

The tree in the corner of the village has been crossed—
has the village been crossed?

The skirt of the newly married bride is wafting—
Hot tears of grief are flowing like a stream.

The poetess indulges in the jugglery of words, but there is no pompous exhibition, presenting high-sounding words. The age-old ideas have been depicted by fitting them into

1. Juara Jeunthi Uthe—p. 30.

the tastes of the modern age with a melodious and sweet undertone—

Abhimāna muñ go kari nahi sakhā
bāḍhi nāhiñ abhijoga,
Śata lānchhana guru apamāna
nirabe karichhi bhoga
Byartha praṇaya mama,
Laksha bāsanā bakshe jharichhi baṇara mālatī sama.[1]

I am not sensitive nor have I
put forth allegations,
I have tolerated hundreds of humiliations
and insults silently.
My frustrated love and
lakhs of desires have withered
Within my heart like wild Mālatī flower.

After the publication '*Juāra Jeuñṭhi Uthe*', the pen of the poetess has gradually become refined and heightened in merit. The poems—'*Tini Adhyāya*', '*Prīti*', *Abhisāra*', '*Niśītha*', *Mahilā Collegera Bedi*', '*Sāhitya,*' '*Praśnavāchi*'. '*Bahnilagnā*', '*Bhāi*', '*Danderaha*', '*Gotie Mruta Jharanāra Kahaṇi*', '*Pratyuttara Gotie Chiṭhira*', '*Viseṣaṇa*', '*Nāri*', '*Gotie Sakālara Kavitā*', '*Viśwa Pārabāra*', '*Kshamā*', '*Chilikā*', '*Dhūlighara*', '*Aśru*' reveal the high idealism and refined conscious personality of the poetess—

Sanskrutira jayagāne sarbanāśī
anartha a mahāsamārohe
Sabhyatāra vijñāpana rāstā ghāte
dokāna bajāre

+ + +

Dhola sama dhauñ dhauñ bāja nahiñ he sabhyatā
śuṇāoni āu jaitranāda,
Bhitaraṭā śūnya khāli, kebala rahichhi bhari
punjibhūta ruddha pratibāda.[1]

1. Juara Jeunthi Uthe—30.
2. Sabhyatara Tale Tale—Samaj, January 26, 1970.

In the victorious songs of culture, in the
pompous and disastrous exhibition of wealth—
The advertisement of civilisation is spread
in the roads and shops.

+ + +

Oh ! civilisation ! do not beat your victorious trumpet
like the rumbling sounds of a drum
You have got only hollowness inside—
with repressed and passive resistance.

Gradually, the pen of the writer tends to become restrained and controlled. She visualises the world to be full of eternal happiness and bliss by the sprinkling of the magic-water of 'all-pervasive forgiveness'—

Bele bele mane hue
Tame sehi urjwasvala vedamaṇtra.
Āryābarta prakampita kari
Sādhanā-smāraka anuṣṭup chhanda.
Mandrita, jhankāra tame pavitra omkāra
śubhra-anabadya.[1]

Sometimes I think--

You are the chants of the intellectual Vedic mantras—
which vibrate through the land of the Aryas—
reminding us of the meditations—
Anustubh metre
You are the sacred 'Om' with a deep rumble
crystal-clear and inimitable.

'Ramyarachanā' is mainly based on emotion or intense feelings. Its constituents and style are subjective. On account of being beautiful (*Ramya*) it is known as *'Ramyarachanā.* I came across such a one,[2] entitled *'Kāchaghara'* by Smt. Mohapatra. The sweet reminiscences of a past collegian are

1. Kshama—Jhankara, 21st year, 10th Number.
2. Jhankara—October, 1968.

painted here. This 'epilogue' of women, who are now the young mothers of school-going children or elderly mothers of officers of rank; mothers of politicians belonging to heterogeneous parties or men holding high places in various phases of society, looks back upon their College days, full of the bright colours of a rainbow and in a vacant and pensive mood, they cast heavy sighs as their imaginative Glass-Houses (*Kāchaghara*) are now broken to pieces by the shocks of realism. The essay is replete with restrained compassion intermingled with an imaginative fervour.

An anthology of short stories named *Pruthivi Śaraśajyā* has been published by the author. The story entitled *Guāghia* is worth mention.

Binapani Mohanty :

Vyāsakavi Fakirmohan Senapati seems to be the first and foremost writer of Oriya short-stories. The story named *Rebatī* depicts the antagonistic views of a conservative old lady towards the ways of modern education.

During the first half of the twentieth century, in most of the Indian languages, was noticed a wide gulf between the regular stock-in-trade short stories of the previous authors, and the ultra-modern short stories written on the basis of the current age and tradition. Usually the settings of such stories are domestic, and even the actions which were supposed to take place in historical times are reviewed and seen through contemporary eyes. The general mass of the new Era want to read everyday problems treated in the short stories and to see heroes and heroines drawn from their own ranks. They want more of action and sentiment rather than long discourses by the various characters. The taste for extravagant and fantastic situations has gained the upper hand and hence such stories are gradually becoming completely eccentric. In this march of neoromanticism, the handmaids of the 'created characters' are materialistic and secular love, and neurosis or psychosis are their guiding principles. Hence the heroines of such stories lose their mental balance and need 'sleeping tablets' or 'tranquillisers' to have eternal sleep. The short story named

'*Sādhāraṇa*' by the contemplative rising young writer Smt. Binapani Mohanty is written in this vein—

"Arati opened the vanity-bag of Latika. In the bag are found a handful of medicines and jumbled up miscellaneous paper-bits. Suddenly she was shocked ! Just an hour ago, in Nandita's house, she saw these medicines which Nandita feels proud of, that she loves them more than Soumendra! —the sleeping tablets !! Soumendra may betray her—everybody else in the world may practise fraud with her—pain her heart —or squeeze out her blood in deception !! But these sleeping tablets ! Oh ! they only provide her tranquillity ! —provide her with the zeal to live life ! At the time of conversing with Nandita, Arati thought—Nandita is a show-piece or she is abnormal ! But Latika also possesses the same tablets ! the same tranquilliser of life ! the same source of zeal for living !"[1]

In the modern world, the worship of 'Money-God' is the only 'rational attitude' ; but in such a worship 'animality' predominates. Soumendra and Sukanta—the dual heroes of *Sādhāraṇa*' are the two burning examples.

Some anthologies of short stories have also been published by Smt. Mohanty, such as '*Navataraṅga*' '*Pānthaśālā O Raktakarabī*', '*Kasturi Mruga O Sabuja Araṇya*'. These stories are a psychological analysis of the different conflicts, complicacies and disillusionments of men brought up in the lap of today's materialistic civilization. The flowing uninhibited style and neat presentation of the stories are noteworthy. In *Chāmelira Chā* the feelings and inner conflicts of an ordinary lower middle-class woman in society have been ploughed successfully to the farthest extent and depicted artistically with a coverage of the necessary 'sentiments'.

The writer's first novel '*Sitāra Śoṇita*' was being published serially in the consecutive issues of 'Asantā Kāli'. It depicts the story of the heroine who though educated in the modern lines of western education still retains the sanctity and chastity of her blood flowing in her veins since the Epic-age of 'Sītā'. She has been wounded and injured by the blows of modern

1. 'Sadharana', Jhankara, 21st year, 10th Edition. (Trans. by me)

civilisation, but till her last breath clings to the age-old idea of chastity in womanhood.

Smt. Mohanty has been recently honoured by the Sahitya Akademi, Orissa branch, for her literary compositions.

Nandini Satpathy :

Smt. Satpathy, in spite of her political career and the heavy responsibilities of a Union Minister has been able to contribute short stories, poems and essays for the growth and development of Oriya literature. Many of them have been translated into Hindi and English. Her anthology of short stories *Ketoṭi Kathā*', illustrates her original endowment grown up, tempered and shaped by experience and judgment. We hope, that through many a rough and uncomfortable days of 'politics' laid ahead, Mrs. Satpathy will not lose touch with the quiet dignity of a creative writer.

Other Authoresses

Psychological perception into the nature of life in which nobility and baseness are intermingled, even in the finest individual, specially in the young men about the city and their nymphs, form the subject-matter of '*Aṅge Aṅge Raṅga Lāge* and '*Bibaraṇa Pruthivī*'—the two novels written by Smt. Bina Mohapatra.

The two novels '*Dūra Diganta*' and '*Adina Megha*', written by the well known social worker Smt. Kuntalakumari Acharya depict characters of romantic loveliness in a sweet undertone. Recently '*Adina Megha*' has been filmed.

Adopting the beauty queen of the city of Vaiśālī as the heroine, Smt. Shanti Mohapatra has written a novel named 'Buddhaṁ Śaraṇaṁ Gachhāmi', completely in a different style. The evening, dropping her veil of darkness over a clandestine meeting of the harlot and her lover is very enjoyable.

The novels '*Paīchha*' and '*Phatā Kāntha*' written by Smt. Khirodra Parija give evidence of social disintegration in the backdrop of pastoral settings.

'*Agraja*' by Smt. Sita Devi Khadanga, '*Hasa Hasa Mora Priya*' and '*Swapnara Samādhi*' by Smt. Labangalata Devi Vidusi, '*Sruṣṭi Pralaya*' by Smt. Kalpanakumari Devi, 'Ete Andhara, Kete Jwāla' by Smt. Kanaklata Mohanty, 'Kia Tume Nārī' by Smt. Kanchanalata Sahu, '*Gotie Sāgara Kotie Dheu*' by Smt. Saudamini Udgata are novels imposing a credible order upon ordinary reality. The two detective novels—'*Saundaryara Mrutyu*' and '*Gupta Ghātaka*' by Smt. Bina Devi are enjoyable.

(Dr.) Smt. Rajeswari Dalabehera, who is a medical practitioner, has also made a name by composing an anthology of short stories entitled—'*Chorā Chaitāli*'. As an expert in scanning the anatomy of a human skeleton, a doctor by profession and a writer by choice she has also been successful in scanning the secret mental recesses of a complicated human heart. Hence such a collection is enjoyable.

In the short story of Smt. Supriti Devi Gantayat, entitled 'Truṣṇā O Taṭinī', she has been able to depict the evils of the modern society, adopting the line of thoughts of 'Albert Camus', as her characters are 'crushed between human evil and destiny'.[1]

The dual feeling of refinement and vulgarity, attraction towards the dazzling earthiness of modern life, the horror of a life without faith in God, the disillusioned weariness of the so-called advanced education, the agonised slow drying up of the springs of tender emotions have been successfully painted in—'*Mruttikā Darśana*' by Smt. Renuka Devi, '*Marama Talara Dheu*' by Smt. Hemalata Mansinha, '*Kuheli*' and '*Sātoṭi Galpa*' by Smt. Usharani Panda, '*Abagunṭhanara Tale*' by Smt. Triveni Devi, '*Galpa Sanchayana*' by Smt. Premalata Dash, '*Truṇāṅkura*' by Smt. Sumitra Devi. Besides these, the short stories of Smt. Shobharani Panda, Smt. Shakuntala Panda, Smt. Nirodprava Patnaik, Smt. Sundaramani Patnaik, Smt. Banaj Devi have been published in various journals. On account of the wide variety of such compositions, it is not possible to find out a definite style or central idea of the concerned authors.

The drama entitled 'Puruṣottamadeva' by Mādhavī Dāsī :

It has been mentioned earlier that the Vaiṣṇavī poetess *Mādhavī Dāsī* composed a drama in Sanskrit entitled

1. 'Truṣṇa O Taṭinī', Jibanaranga, Sravana 1374, August issue.

'Puruṣottama Deva'. She seems to be the first and foremost Oriya woman-writer, whose compositions have been preserved in palm-leaf manuscripts.

The story of the drama runs thus—

Emperor Puruṣottama Deva ascended the throne of Kaliṅga after the death of his father Emperor Kapilendra Deva. The Gajapati king Puruṣottama Deva fell in love with Padmāvatī, the beautiful daughter of the king of Kanchi. "The Raja of Kanchi was a great devotee of Ganapati. He refused to give his daughter in marriage to Puruṣottama, who used to do the sweeper's work before the image of Jagannath during the Car Festival. Puruṣottama marched at the head of a large army against the Raja of Kanchi to avenge the slight cast upon him and his God. It is said that Jagannath and Balaram took part in the expedition in the guise of horsemen. Puruṣottama took the citadel of Kanchi and married the daughter of the Raja of Kanchi".[1]

The number of women-dramatists who have composed dramas in Sanskrit language are meagre, as Sanskrit is a very difficult language to master and drama moreover is—'one of the greatest mediums of human expression'.

Unfortunately, these highly stylised Sanskrit dramas fell into evil days after the Muslim invasion. The absence of patronage from the ruling Muslim kings handicapped the creativeness and enthusiasm of the dramatists to present stage productions. At such a juncture of the decadence period of Sanskrit dramas, sprang up the different regional languages in the different states of the then India. Sanskrit drama was reborn under these changed conditions, being written and produced in the various regional languages. The rigid and vigorous rules of the forms of composition of the Sanskrit dramas were given up in the course of this re-birth in the life-circle of dramas.

The first Oriya play, named *'Kānchi Kāverī'* was written by Sri Ramshankar Ray in 1888 A. D. It was a historical play.

1. The story of 'Puruṣottama Deva' is historically corroborated by Prof. P. Mukherjee in his 'The Gajapati Kings of Orissa' p. 60.

Gradually 'social plays' replaced 'historical and mythological plays' according to the changed outlook and needs of society.

But Oriya literature has very little contribution to this branch from the women-dramatists of Orissa. A full-fledged drama under the caption—'*Janma Tithi*' composed by Smt. Sita Devi Khadanga is worth mention.

Keeping pace with the 'fast life' of the modern age, dramas of great length have been replaced by short 'one-act' plays. In the struggle for existence, a distinctly utilitarian or practical outlook has developed. The one-act plays composed in regional languages broadcast from the All India Radio centres are providing popular entertainment in a distinctly scheduled period of time. At no time in our history has there been so much production of plays as the one-act plays of the present day. The women writers, who have composed radio-plays to their credit are—Smt. Sarla Devi, Smt. Manorama Mohapatra, Smt. Bina Devi, Smt. Binapani Mohanty, Smt. Pratimarani Bastia, Smt. Basantakumari Patnaik and Smt. Manojmanjari Das.

Times are constantly changing ; so also the tastes of the people in general. To quote Martin Esslin "The theatre of the Absurd has become a catch-phrase, much used and much abused. What does it stand for? Perhaps it will be best to answer the second question first. There is no organised movement, no school of artists, who claim the label for themselves"[1] In continuation, he writes—"A term like Theatre of the Absurd must therefore be understood as a kind of intellectual shorthand for a complex pattern of similarities in approach, method, and convention of shared philosophical and artistic premises, whether conscious or subconscious and of influences from a common store of tradition".[2] This school of Absurd Drama is gradually gaining popularity.

Criticisms and Dissertations:

"It is a part of the business of the critic to see literature steadily and to see it whole; and this is entirely essential to see

1. Absurd Drama by Martin Esslin, p. 1.
2. ibid.

is not consecrated by time, to see the best work of our time and the best work of twenty-five years ago with the same eyes".[1]

'Criticism' as defined above has not yet stepped into the pen of women-writers of Orissa. Among the dissertations— 'Adhunika Sikshita' by Dr. Suryamani Devi, 'Alankara and Alankara-tattva' by Smt. Labanya Nayak are to be mentioned. Besides these books, the essays in different journals and weeklies have come into prominence from the pens of such women-writers as Smt. Shova Ray, Smt. Shanti Nanda, Smt. Shanti Misra, Smt. Ketaki Nayak, Smt. Purnalata Misra, Smt. Kananbala Tripathy, Smt.Nirmala Panda, Smt. Vasabadutta Misra, Smt. Mihirkumari Mohanty, Smt. Binapani Mohanty, Smt. Kanaklata Mohapatra, Smt. Banoj Devi, Smti. Sujata Priyambada, Smt. Sulekha Das, Smt. Basantalata, Mohanty, Smt. Kumudini Acharya, Smt. Kanaklata Sinha, Smt. Manorama Mohapatra. Smt. Giribala Mohanty, Smt. Radharani Patnaik, Smt. Belarani Chand, Smt. Manorama Biswal, Smt. Kiranabala Misra, Smt. Vijayini Patnaik, Smt. Sanjukta Das etc.

The dissertations of Smt. Shanno Devi regarding religion and religious literature are enjoyable. '*Sachitrā, Rāṁāyaṇa*' and '*Pūrṇa Sāra*' by Smt. Annapurna Misra provide a sweet reading.

Translations:

The following works have been translated into Oriya from their originals—

Smt. Annapurna Maharana has translated Sri Narahari Parikh's '*Taruni Kanyā Prati*' and *Strīpuruṣa Maryādā*'. Smt. Sita Devi Khadanga has translated poet Rabindranath Tagore's '*Ghare Baire*', Smt. Shanti Devi has translated '*Lauha Kapāṭ*' by Jarasandha. Premchand's *Nārī Jiban kī Kahāniā*' and '*Nirmalā*' have been respectively translated by Smt. Nihar Mohapatra and Smt. Uma Dash. Smt. Nalini Devi Routray and Smt. Soudamini Udgata (Ashalata) have also translated some compositions into Oriya. Louis Fisher's famous book on Gandhiji

1. (i) Introduction to Sacred Wood.
(ii) The achievement of T. S. Eliot by F. O. Matthissen, p. 1.

has been translated by Smt. Shanti Patnaik as *'Bāpu jibanī O Sandeś.*

Travelogues:

'*America Chithī*' by the young writer Smt. Ramarani Misra provides a delightful reading. Specially the true-to-life experiences of the author about the social ideals, economic forms and political principles of a country like the United States of America, said to be in possession of fabulous riches, are compassiontely painted. '*Americara Ghara O Gharaṇī*' by Smt.Kumudini Mohapatra is also equally enjoyable by the housewives of Orissa.

Juvenile Literature

The pen of women derived its first inspiration in composing lullabies and nursery rhymes for the children; like the circumference of a circle the women writers of Orissa have finalised their efforts in 'Juvenile Literature' for in no other branch have the women of Orissa been rewarded for their compositions in all India level, except in 'children's literature'.

Smt. Bidyutprave Devi, Smt. Basantakumari Patnaik, Smt, Kananbala Tripathy, Smt. Punyaprava Devi, Smt. Sitamani Devi, Smt. Monorama Mohapatra and the like have written books specifically for the use of children. '*Jāhāku Jia*' and *Kañalā Jibana*' by Smt. Bidyutprava, '*Hīrā Moti Māṇika*' by Smt. Kananbala and '*Galare Galā Kāḷia Baḷada*' by Smt. Punyaprava have been rewarded by the Government of India.

Not only in the field of literature, but also women have contributed to the field of kitchen and other household needs of life. *Bibidha Randhana Sīkshā*' by Smt. Kuntalakumari, '*Sahaja Randhana Sīkshā*' by Smt. Arati Devi, a book on 'Sewing and Tailoring' by Smt. S. Samal, a book on 'Knitting' by Smt. Amiya Mohapatra and '*Mahilā Samabāya Sikshā*' by Smt. Binita Roy are worth mention.

Journals edited by women:

Smt. Padmalaya Dash, a member of the Advisory Board

of the Sahitya Akademy (Centre) has dedicated herself to the publication of various articles, after translating them into English from Oriya. This ensures the diffusion and spread of Oriya literature in other States. She is also a Reporter-cum-Journalist of prominent English newspapers.

In the year 1902, Smt. Reba Roy edited a paper, entitled '*Prabhat*'. In 1937, Smt. Sharatkumari Hazra revived the publication of '*Prabhat*', which in the meantime had gone into oblivion. After seven years of continuous service, 'Prabhat' also dropped off. '*Samāj Kalyāṇa*' by Smt. Nalini Devi Routray and 'Yuganārī' by Dr. (Smt.) Radha Devi were also being published sometime ago. The monthly magazine '*Sourava*' containing good literary articles is being published now regularly by Smt. Bina Mohapatra.

Ultra-modernism in Literature:

Now-a-days we often come across the phrase 'Ultra-modernism in Literature'. To some it seems more like a subtle disease, than like an advance into freedom and light.

"It would be easy to abandon the literary discipline, with an easy sense of liberation, to those who are victims of an artistic fallacy and who hold that the literature of the past exists in our minds alone and that it is and can only be what we choose to make it, or that what it ought to say is more significant than what in fact it says. The present century is tragically familiar with systems of tyranny that offer themselves as liberation, and the doctrine of an eternal present in literature is a freedom little better than theirs".[1]

Today's literature depicts a great gulf between yesterday and today. This attitude has come up out of a feeling of 'Frustration', experienced by the modern youth. Social inequality is giving rise to a crude and negligent state of mind, leading to snobbery and snobbery to frustration. Commenting on this, one of the eminent personalities of Orissa, Dr. H. K. Mahtab states—"The root cause of frustration is that the writer is not getting a place anywhere according to his

1. The Study of Literature by George Warton, p. 220.
2. Jhankar, 20th year, 11th Edition—Editorial. (Trans. by me)

own satisfacation. Getting a place means—a desire in one's mind—an insinuation of the mind. But in order to get this desire fulfilled, the body, the mind, and the soul must work in collaboration. If we are not prepared to gather the mental strength which is required for its achievement, then necessarily we will get frustration. Then we will think, let everything—every culture and civilization be crushed. This world and this life are but full of 'sound and fury signifying nothing'. Human mind is not prepared to accept a literature which has been created out of this sort of "Frustration".[1]

The modern literary trend has evolved without any specified 'Manifesto' and is silently creeping into vogue. The reasons as to why this has occurred and the conditions governing the new situation are still open to debate. Kafka, a novelist, whom one might have expected to feel himself in profound harmony with the new doctrines, wrote in his diary in a hostile spirit "that self-awareness can only be an evil—"psychology is impatience, all human mistakes are impatience, a premature breaking off from the methodical".

The new horizon for women:

Besides opening new avenues for the women-writers in the literary field, the broadcast of Narimahal programmes from the A. I. R., Cuttack, Sambalpur and Jeypore and special 'Lipīka' curriculum have provided opportunities for the women, having a literary bent of mind, to demonstrate their talents.

To quote Prof. Humayun Kabir—"The women of India are fortunate for they have inherited the traditions of both the East and the West. The challenge which awaits them is to translate into reality the ideas and ideals they have thus inherited".[2]

Mrs. Indira Gandhi corroborates the previous statement of Prof. Kabir by saying—"We need strong-mindedness in our country. In all its aspects, India is a complex country. But if I would have to characterise the women of my country, I must say that one quality is common to all of them—they are

1. Jhankar, 20th year, 11th Edition, Editorial. (Trans. by me)
2. Indian Philosophy of Education by Humayun Kabir—p. 55.

strong-minded. They are considered as Shakti or forces of Men".

Hence, our motto, in the present circumstances, should not be to think in the parallel lines of Shelley—

"We look before and after,
And pine for what is not;
Our sincerest laughter with some pain is fraught".

There should be a clarion call to the women of Orissa to build an 'Era' for themselves, where there will be judicious distribution of Indian culture without having any distinction of male or female sex.

EPILOGUE

Mādhavī Dāsī—(earliest Oriya poetess)
(A poem) Language—Brajabhāṣā or Brajaboli
Script—Bengali
(Reproduced in Devanāgarī Script)

आनन्दे नाचत सङ्गे भकत
गौर किशोर—राज ।
भागु उझलि करे फेलाफेलि
नीलाचल—पुरी माझ ।।
शुनिया नागरी प्रमेते आगरि
धाइया चलिल वाटे ।
हेरिया गौरे पड़िया फांफरे
दूरे थाकि देखे नाटे ।।
दुवाहु तुलिया वेड़ाय नाचिया
भकत—गणेक सङ्ग ।
नीलाचल—वासी मने अभिलाषी
कौतुके देखिये रङ्ग ।।
बाजे करताल बोले भलि भाल
आर बाजे ताहे खोल ।।
माधवि दास मनेते उल्लास
सदा बले हरिबोल ।।

Bibliography

1. Oriya Sahityara Parichaya
By **B. C. Mazumdar**
2. Oriya Sahityara Krama Parinama (Parts I, II, III)
Pandit Nilakantha Das
3. Oriya Ṣahityara Itihasa (Parts I, II, III)
Pandit Suryanarayana Dash
4. Oriya Sahityara Itihasa
Dr. Mayadhara Mansinha
5. Oriya Sahityara Itihasa
Dr. Natabara Samantaraya
6. Oriya Sahityara Itihasa (Part I)
Sri Brundabanachandra Acharya
7. Adhunika Oriya Sahityara Itihasa
Pandit Vinayak Misra
8. Oriya Lokageeta O Kahani
Dr. Kunjabehari Dash
9. Adhunika Sahityara Bhumi O Bhumika
(A compilation) **Dr. Kunjabehari Dash**
10. Adhunika Oriya Sahityara Bhittibhumi
Dr. Natahar Samantaraya
11. Bharatiya Sahitya Sastra (Part I)
Pandit Baldev Upadhyaya

Essays

1. Orissare Nari Pratibha
Oriya Sahitya Samikshana—Part I
Dr. Bichitrananda Mohanti

2. Adhunika Oriya Sahitya O Nari Lekhani
Jhankara—20th year, 11th Edition
Smt. Binapani Mohanti.

Magazines

Jhankara, Jibanaranga, Kshanika
(Radhanatha Visesanka)

Manuscript

Orissara Parba-Parbani
Orissa State Museum

NOTE : The years 1317, 1340 etc. used under the "Modern period" in this book are known as Dillisvar abda (era of the emperor of Delhi) which is prevalent in Orissa, even to-day along with other Eras.